AF474618

the furtwängler sound

seventh edition of the discography

this volume is dedicated to
the memory of
maisie woodard 1920-2014

compiled by john hunt

The Furtwängler Sound
Seventh Edition of the Discography

John Hunt

ISBN 978-1-901395-30-3

Travis & Emery Music Bookshop
17 Cecil Court
London
WC2N 4EZ
United Kingdom.
Tel. (+44) (0) 20 7240 2129.
newpublications@travis-and-emery.com

Contents

The Furtwängler Sound: introduction to the seventh edition

When in 1982 I first produced a discography of Wilhelm Furtwängler (1886-1954), my only predecessor in the field had been the Danish scholar Henning Smidth Olsen (1970/updated 1973). That 1973 revision in its distinctive red cover was to remain a reliable guide for the Furtwängler completist as well as a solid source for all the later listings which were to appear both in Europe and the Far East. In more recent times these have been joined by various online discographies.

"The Furtwängler Sound" was itself incorporated into two important reference works about the conductor, "Furtwängler: Analyse, Dokument und Protokoll" by Joachim Matzner (Atlantis-Verlag 1986) and "The Furtwängler Record" by John Ardoin (Amadeus Press 1994) before continuing into further independent editions up to and including the sixth one in 1999. I must add that in all this work I was given constant encouragement by the conductor's indefatigable widow Elisabeth, who is sadly no longer here to endorse this seventh version of the discography.

Regular readers will recall that I was initially sceptical about a chronological listing and preferred one which was alphabetical by composer and therefore more user-friendly to the general reader. However, more recent work on the discographies of various orchestras has convinced me of certain merits to this approach: the discography is therefore in chronological format, followed by a composer listing cross-referenced to the main section. I have also been won over to the inclusion of matrix numbers for the 78rpm recordings: these can be helpful in clarifying the sequence in which a recording was made, although in the case of the pre-war Polydor recordings reasoned logic does not appear to have been a priority in the allocation of such numbers! It also has to be borne in mind that in the last days of the shellac era, when tape recording had already been introduced in anticipation of the new LP format, matrix numbers were sometimes allocated but never actually used.

introduction/contined

Research in the intervening years has also enabled me to be more precise about recording dates as well as venues, and in some cases has even exended to being able to identify the recording producer or sound engineer. All this information is contained in a headiing with a session number (followed in brackets by the original Olsen numbers for the works in that session). The afore-mentioned 78rpm matrix numbers then appear in the left-hand column, followed in a second column by the 78rpm catalogue number (two matrrix numbers for the two sides of the shellac disc). There then ensue the main re-issues in 45rpm, LP, reel-to-reel tape, CD and occasional video formats, as well as most recently some editions which are available as downloads. What I have not included are the Japanese issue numbers for the major record labels EMI and Deutsche Grammophon with prefixes like WF, TOCE and POCG. Many of the recording groups are rounded off with my personal comments about a best edition, but I cannot emphasise too heavily that any such recommendation is entirely subjective.

Over the years we have encountered our fair share of "fake" recordings, usually the result of over-avid research by collectors with a desire to extend Furtwängler's recorded repertoire, like Dvorak's *New World* Symphony. Certain items which were included in Olsen's original discography as being preserved in so-called "private archives" have never been traced: as it seems unlikely that they are going to surface after forty or more years, I have not listed them. They are Olsen numbers 023 (Tchaikovsky 6/1932), 057-058 (Wagner Tannhäuser and Siegfried extracts/1940), 062-063 (Beethoven Concerto 4 and Leonore 3/1941), 097-098 (Beethoven 4 & 5/1944), 114 (Brahms 1/1947), 132 (Beethoven Egmont/1948), 146 (Beethoven 4/1949), 148 (Mozart 40/1949), 166 (Beethoven 9/1949), 171 (Beethoven Fidelio/1949), 183 (Handel op 6 no 5/1950), 204 (Schubert 9/1950), 228 (Schubert 8/1950), 263 (Brahms 4/1951) and 272 (Beethoven 9 finale/1951).

introduction/continued

Other unpublished Furtwängler recordings which cannot completely be overlooked include the 1938 Covent Garden Wagner *Ring* cycle, of which only a small part seems to have survived (Sessions nos. 034 and 035). Although we do possess complete cycles from 1950 and 1953, as well as more extended fragments from the 1937 production, I recall our appetites being whetted by a 1972 article by Ward Botsford in *The American Record Guide,* from which I quote:-

"The Futwängler *Ring* has always been legendary, not least because of the celebrated 1938 Covent Garden production, Covent Garden's overlord at that time, Sir Thomas Beecham, had the entire season preserved on a type of optical film which allowed for a long-play effect if not for extended frequency response. The fate of these films (actually sound recordings), which include not only the two complete *Ring* cycles but also the Beecham-directed *Don Giovanni* and an *Elektra* with Rosa Pauly, is shrouded in mystery. There was talk at one time of their being issued by EMI, but nothing ever came of it. Two magnetic tape copies, made shortly after the war, are presently in the hands of prominent collectors in England and the United States. The original films are (or were, until four years ago) in the possession of the Beecham estate and stored in a warehouse in, of all places, Brooklyn NY. Should any of our more exuberant readers have notions of liberating historic documents, I must warn them that the films, made of cellulose nitrate, are, after all these years, literally explosive. To forestall requests for the identity and whereabouts of the warehouse and the collectors who possess tapes of the Covent Garden *Ring,* let me state here that such inquiries will go unanswered. I shall submit this much, however: the cast of these two performances in London reads like a *Who's who?* of the era's Wagnerian singers: Frida Leider, Maria Müller, Max Lorenz, Ludwig Weber. Lauritz Melchior, Kirsten Flagstad, Franz Völker, Rudolf Bockelmann. Just think about that for a moment!"

As so much of the surviving Furtwängler material before 1945 derives from radio broadcasts, some background information on Germany's broadcasting structure up to that date might be useful During the course of the years 1923-1924 regional broadasting companies had been established, based in the centres Berlin, Leipzig, Munich, Frankfurt-am-Main, Hamburg-Bremen, Stuttgart, Breslau, Königsberg and Münster. Then on 1 May 1925 these stations were brought together into an umbrella organisation known as the *Reichs-Rundfunk-Gesellschaft* (re-named *Grossdeutscher Rundfunk* on 1 January 1939). An additional natuonwide programme, known as *Deutschlandsender,* was broadcast on long wave frequencies. After 1933, and as the National Socialist government embarked on its programme of territorial expansion, additional broadcasting stations were incorporated into the network, primarily *Reichssender Saarbrücken* (1935) and *Reichssender Wien* (1938).

Rapid advances in the use of magnetic tape meant that the broadcasting authorities were particularly keen to enlist Wilhelm Furtwängler's participation in their concert relays (and recordings) from the Berlin *Philharmonie.* The conductor, however, was notoriously sceptical about any form of mechanical reproduction but was won over by the musical and non-interventionalist qualities of the sound engineer Friedrich Schnapp, who supervised the majority of his broadcasts, even accompanying him to other centres like Vienna and Hamburg. The story of how the surviving tapes were seized by the Russians when they entered Berlin in 1945, then transported back to the Soviet Union and eventually published, is by now well-known.

introduction/continued

Early in 1946 the British Decca company, represented by conductor Sidney Beer, approached Wilhelm Furtwängler with the offer of recordings in London with the National Symphony Orchestra, but these negotiations, as well as the first approach from EMI's Walter Legge, were scuppered by the fact that the conductor had not yet been officially de-nazified (Furtwängler had already recorded for EMI's German branch in 1937-1938). It was not until the late autumn of 1947 that Legge succeeded in setting up sessions for him with the *Wiener Philharmoniker* in Vienna, where Legge was already recording Herbert von Karajan. And it was Legge's championing of the younger Austrian conductor which meant that his working relationship with Furtwängler, although fruitful, proved to be less than an easy ride, to the extent that later Vienna recording sessions were supervised by the reliable Lawrance Collingwood. Nevertheless, the *Tristan und Isolde* sessions in London with the Philharmonia Orchestra in 1952 (session no. 194) were produced by Legge with results that drew unstinted praise from the conductor.

I do not pretend to be an expert on computer downloading, but have drawn attention in this new discography to some of those recorded versions of Furtwängler performances which are increasingly becoming available as downloads as opposed to being in the conventional sound-carrier formats. Primarly these are the Pristine Audio label and Chibas Resorations (the latter accessible from www.furtwanglersound.com). And attention should also be drawn to the unofficial Membran label, whose transfers can vary widely in quality from excellent to mediocre: as well as their CD-sets which I have listed, there is apparently a 107-CD compendium which purports to include at least one version of every work which Furtwängler ever recorded.

The main event to which the Furtwängler collector can look forward is a complete edition of its HMV catalogue from Warner Classics: since taking over from EMI, Warner has done excellent work on re-publishing the entire corpus of its back catalogue of Furtwängler's arch rival Herbert von Karajan with remarkable results eclipsing any previous EMI CD re-issues. We can in time only anticipate the same treatment for Wilhelm Furtwängler.

With the work leading up to this seventh edition I have to acknowledge the very active help of my colleague John Baker, as well as thanking again all the many experts and enthusiasts who have supported me in one way or another with this and all previous editions of the discography.

John Hunt 2015

001 (001 and 002)/16-30 october 1926/polydor sessions in berlin

philharmonisches orchester berlin

weber der freischütz overure

172bm 66466

173bm

lp issues: japan JP 1101-1102/discocorp RR 431

cd issues: symposium 1043/dante LYS 116/koch 3-7059-2/japanese furtwängler society WFJ 18/WFJ 22/naxos 8.111003/andromeda ANDRCD 5008

beethoven symphony no 5 in c minor op 67

174bm 69855/brunswick 25005

175bm

216bm 69856/brunswick 25006

217bm

218bm 69857/brunswick 25007

179bm

330 1/2 bm 69858/brunswick 25008

214bm

215bm 69859/brunswick 25009

lp issues: japan NA 122-123/discocorp RR 431/british furtwängler society FURT 100

cd issues: koch 3-7059-2/japanese furtwängler society WFJ 18/japanese furtwängler centre WFHC 021-022/naxos 8.111003/andromeda ANDRCD 5008

WFHC 021-022 contains versions of the symphony taken from both polydor and brunswickpressings

These very first attempts to record Wilhelm Furtwängler in front of an orchestra, using the early electrical method of "Lichtstrahl" (beam of light method), were only moderately successful.
Most efforts to transfer the recordings to LP and then CD have also had limited success, and only the most recent Naxos transfers can be described as making the rare originals worthwhile as an experience for modern listeners.

002 (003-006 and 014)/13 june 1929/polydor session in berlin hochschule für musik

philharmonisches orchester berlin

mendelssohn ein sommernachtstraum overture

857bi I 66925/69206/brunswick 90137

858bi I

859bi I 66926/69207/brunswick 90138

lp issues: heliodor 88 021/deutsche grammophon 2535 821

cd issues: dante LYS 116/documents 20 3090/20 3093/223 508/koch 3-7073-2/ french furtwängler society SWF 042-043/naxos 8.111004/andromeda ANDRCD 5008

bach air from orchestral suite no 3 BWV 1068

860bi I 66926/66935/95418/brunswick 90050/decca CA 8014

45 rpm issue: deutsche grammophon EPL 30 164

lp issues: deutsche grammophon LPEM 19 078/2535 827/japan JP 1101-1102

cd issues: music and arts CD 954/koch 3-7059-2/documents 223 508/french furtwängler society SWF 042-044/naxos 8.111136/andromeda ANDRCD 5008/ japanese furtwängler society WFJ 15-16

schubert ballet music no 2 from the incidental music to rosamunde D797

861bi 66935/95458/brunswick 90050/decca CA 8098

45 rpm issue: deutsche grammophon EPL 30 164

lp issue: heliodor 88 021

cd issues: symposium 1043/palladio PD 4176/dante LYS 114/documents 20 3090/ 20 3093/223 508/koch 3-7059-2/french furtwängler society SWF 042-044/ naxos 8.111136/deutsche grammophon 477 5238/andromeda ANDRCD 5008

schubert entr'acte no 3 from the incidental music to rosamunde D797

862bi 95418/95458/brunswick 90162/decca CA 8098

lp issues: heliodor 88 021/japan AT 05-06

cd issues: symposium 1043/palladio PD 4176/dante LYS 114/documents 20 3090/ 20 3093/223 508/koch 3-7059-2/french furtwängler society SWF 042-044/ naxos 8.111136/andromeda ANDRCD 5008

matrix number 862bi was re-dubbed for some issues as 1102 1/2bi I: it was at one stage incorrectly thought that these were two separate recordings

The Naxos edition is the easiest way to access these performances, but an even more remarkable restoration process has been carried out by the French Furtwängler Society

003/12 august 1929/polydor session in berlin hochschule für musik

philharmonisches orchester berlin

brahms hungarian dance no 3 in f

1648 1/2 bh I unpublished

1649 1/2 bh I

cd issue: japanese furtwängler society WFJ 18

according to rene tremine this ten-inch disc was discovered as recently as 1995 and was incorrectly labelled as hungarian dance no 1

004 (007-013 and 015-018)/6 january, 7 february and 5 june 1930/ polydor sessions in berlin hochschule für musik

philharmonisches orchester berlin

wagner lohengrin prelude

1085 1/2 bi I 95408/91030/brunswick 90231/decca CA 8089

1086 3/4 bi I

lp issues: heliodor 88021/top classic TC 9054

cd issues: documents 20 3090/20 3092/223 508/koch 3-7073-2/french furtwängler society SWF 042-043/naxos 8.111005/andromeda ANDRCD 5008/ archipel ARPCD 0261

wagner tristan und isolde prelude

1087 1/2 bi I 95438/91028/brunswick 90201/decca CA 8039

1088 1/2 bi I

1089bi I 95439/91029/brunswick 90202/decca CA 8156

lp issue: 88021

cd issues: koch 3-7073-2/french furtwängler society SWF 042-043/ naxos 8.111005/andromeda ANDRCD 5008

wagner tristan und isolde liebestod, orchestral arrangement

1089bi I 95439/91029/brunswick 90202/decca CA 8156

1090 1/2 bi I

45 rpm issue: deutsche grammophon EPL 30 540

lp issue: heliodor 88 021

cd issues: koch 3-7073-2/french furtwängler society SWF 042-044/ naxos 8.111005/andromeda ANDRCD 5008

004/continued

schubert rosamunde overture D644
1091bi I brunswick 90147
1092bi I
lp issues: british furtwängler society FURT 100/japan JP 1101-1102/AT 05-06
cd issues: symposium 1043/palladio PD 4176/dante LYS 114/documents 20 3090/20 3092/223 508/french furtwängler society SWF 042-044/ koch 3-7059-4/naxos 8.111136/andromeda ANDRCD 5008

strauss till eulenspiegels lustige streiche: rehearsal sequences
1093bi unpublished
1094bi
lp issues: deutsche grammophon 2740 260/japan AT 13-14/french furtwängler society SWF 7906
cd issue: french furtwängler society SWF 042-044

strauss till eulenspiegels lustige streiche
1095 1/2 bi I 95410/91024/decca CA 8053
1096 1/2 bi I
1097bi I 95411/91025/decca CA 8054
lp issues: rococo 2014/japan JP 1101-1102/deutsche grammophon 2740 260
cd issues: arlecchino ARL 111-112/documents 20 3090/20 3093/223 508/ koch 3-7073-2/french furtwängler society SWF 042-044/naxos 8.111005/ andromeda ANDRCD 5008

mendelssohn die hebriden overture
1098bi I 95470/brunswick 90401/decca CA 8090
1099bi I
lp issues: heliodor 88 012/deutsche grammophon 2535 821
cd issues: grammofono AB 78574/dante LYS 116/koch 3-7073-2/deutsche grammophon 477 5238/french furtwängler society SWF 042-044/naxos 8.111004/ andromeda ANDRCD 5008/japanese furtwängler society WFFC 1406

mendelssohn die hebriden overture: rehearsal sequence
1100bi I unpublished
cd issues: tahra FURT 1008-1011/french furtwängler society SWF 042-044/ deutsche grammophon 477 5238

004/continued

berlioz marche hongroise from la damnation de faust

1101 1/2 bi I 95411/91025/decca CA 8054

lp issue: heliodor 88 021

cd issues: koch 3-7073-2/french furtwängler society SWF 042-044/naxos 8.111004/ andromeda ANDRCD 5008/japanese furtwängler society WFJ 15-16

dvorak slavonic dance op 46 no 3

1103bi unpublished

cd issues: tahra FURT 1008-1011/french furtwängler society SWF 042-044/ deutsche grammophon 477 5238

bach brandenburg concerto no 3 in g BWV 1048

1104bi I 95417/brunswick 90161/decca CA 8013

1105 1/2 bi I

1106 3/4 bi I 95418/brunswick 90162/decca CA 8014

45rpm issue: deutsche grammophon EPL 30 539

lp issues: deutsche grammophon 2535 827/discocorp RR 431

cd issues: symposium 1043/grammofono AB 78574/dante LYS 117/music and arts CD 954/membran 20.3090/20.3093/223 508/koch 3-7059-2/french furtwängler society SWF 042-044/naxos 8.111136/andromeda ANDRCD 5008/ japanese furtwängler society WFJ 15-16

rossini la gazza ladra overture

1108 1/2 bi I 95427/91021/brunswick 90188/decca CA 8055

1109 1/2 bi I

lp issues: heliodor 88 021/japan AT 13-14

cd issues: grammofono AB 78574/dante LYS 116/music and arts CD 954/ membran 20.3090/20.3093/223 508/koch 3-7059-2/french furtwängler society SWF 042-044/naxos 8.111003/andromeda ANDRCD 5008/ japanese furtwängler society WFJ 15-16

004/concluded

brahms hungarian dances nos 1 in g minor and 10 in e

2580 1/2 bi I 90190/brunswick 85034/decca DE 7006

2587 1/2 bi I

lp issues: heliodor 88021/melodiya D 030275-030276

cd issues: symposium 1043/dante LYS 204/koch 3-7073-2/membran 223 508/ deutsche grammophon 477 5238/french furtwängler society SWF 042-044/ naxos 8.111005/andromeda ANDRCD 5008/japanese furtwängler society WFJ 15-16

78rpm issues of hungarian dance no 10 were incorrectly described as hungarian dance no 3

French Furtwängler Society SWF 042-044 is highly recommended for maximum appreciation of the music recorded at session 004: it is also the only edition to include all items (including the previously unpublished tracks)

005/28 march 1930/concert recording in hamburg musikhalle

philharmonisches orchester berlin

hindemith konzertmusik

unpublished recording of this world premiere performance described by rene tremine as being in the possession of deutsches rundfunkarchiv

006 (019)/16 june 1930/concert recording in berlin philharmonie

philharmonisches orchester berlin

beethoven symphony no 9: second movement

unpublished recording numbered RRG 937-9

007 (020)/23 july 1931/stage recording in bayreuth festspielhaus

orchester der bayreuther festspiele/nanny larsen-todsen/anny helm/ lauritz melchior

wagner tristan und isolde: begehrt herrin was ihr wünscht!; act two prelude; hörst du sie noch?; dein werk o törige magd!; sie zu löschen zag' ich nicht

unpublished acetate broadcast recordings

008 (020 and 021)/18 august 1931/stage recording in bayreuth festspielhaus

chor und orchester der bayreuther festspiele/nanny larsen-todsen/ anny helm/gotthelf pistor/rudolf bockelmann

wagner tristan und isolde: elend im sterben lag; so reihte sie die mutter; müht euch die?

unpublished acetate broadcast recordings

lp issue: danacord DACO 131-133

cd issue: istituto discografico italiano IDIS 330-331

act one prelude from this performance may also have been published on the acanta label

009 (024)/15 march 1932/concert recording in berlin philharmonie

philharmonisches orchester berlin

brahms symphony no 3: fourth movement

unpublished radio recording numbered BLN 203.1505-7

010 (025)/17 april 1932/dress rehearsal recording in berlin philharmonie

wilhelm furtwängler speaks on the occasion of the orchestra's fiftieth anniversary

unpublished radio recording numbered BLN 204.1701

011 (026)/18 april 1932/concert recording in berlin philharmonie
philharmonisches orchester berlin/bruno-kittel-chor/ria ginster/
frieda dieroff/helge rosvaenge/rudolf bockelmann
beethoven symphony no 9 "choral": unspecified excerpts
unpublished radio recording numbered BLN 204.1801-4

012 (027)/17 october 1932/concert recording in berlin philharmonie
philharmonisches orchester berlin
reger variations and fugue on a theme of mozart: fugue
unpublished radio recording numbered BLN 210.1701-3

013 (028)/27 october 1932/concert recording in berlin philharmonie
philharmonisches orchester berlin/szymon goldberg/paul hindemith
mozart sinfonia concertante K364: third movement
unpublished radio recording numbered BLN 210.2701-2

014 (029)/20 december 1932/concert recording in berlin philharmonie
philharmonisches orchester berlin
beethoven symphony no 8: second and third movements
unpublished radio recording numbered BLN 212.2001-3

015 (022)/december 1932/polydor session in berlin hochschule für musik

philharmonisches orchester berlin

weber-berlioz aufforderung zum tanz

631 1/2 be 67056/brunswick 90313

632be I

lp issues: heliodor 88 021/deutsche grammophon 2535 821/ melodiya D 030275-030276

cd issues: dante LYS 116/koch 3-7073-2/naxos 8.111004/french furtwängler society SWF 042-044/andromeda ANDRCD 5008

016 (034)/6 february 1933/concert recording in berlin philharmonie

philharmonisches orchester berlin

tchaikovsky symphony no 5: part of second movement

unpublished radio recording numbered BLN 302.0606-4

017 (035)/15 november 1933/concert recording in berlin philharmonie

philharmonisches orchester berlin

beethoven egmont overture

unpublished radio recording numbered RRG 311.1501-3

018 (030-033)/november 1933/polydor sessions in berlin hochschule für musik

philharmonisches orchester berlin

wagner götterdämmerung: trauermusik

733be I 67054/91026/brunswick 90251/decca CA 8173

734 1/2 be I

lp issues: heliodor 88 021/deutsche grammophon 2700 703/2721 113/ melodiya D 033213-033214

cd issues: symposium 1043/membran 20.3090/20.3092/223 508/ koch 3-7073-2/deutsche grammophon 477 5238/naxos 8.111136/ french furtwängler society SWF 042-044/andromeda ANDRCD 5008

beethoven egmont overture

735be I 67055/brunswick 90250/decca CA 8170

736be I

45rpm issue: deutsche grammophon EPL 30 540

lp issues: deutsche grammophon 2535 827/japan JP 110-112

cd issues: symposium 1043/grammofono AB 78574/dante LYS 074/ membran 20.3090/20.3093/225 308/deutsche grammophon 453 7002/ 453 8042/koch 3-7059-2/french furtwängler society SWF 042-044/ naxos 8.111003/andromeda ANDRCD 5008

mozart le nozze di figaro and die entführung aus dem serail overtures

737be I 35013/45130/brunswick 90402/decca CA 8187

738 1/2 be I

45rpm issue: deutsche grammophon EPL 30 172

lp issues: deutsche grammophon LPM 18 960/2535 827/ heliodor (usa) H 25079/HS 25079

cd issues: symposium 1043 (figaro only)/dante LYS 117/deutsche grammophon 431 8732/ membran 20.3090 (figaro only)/20.3093 (figaro only)/225 308 (figaro only)/koch 3-7059-2/french furtwängler society SWF 042-044/naxos 8.111136/andromeda ANDRCD 5008

The recommended CD version for the items in Session 018 remains French Furtwängler Society SWF 042-044

019 (036-038)/may-june 1935/polydor sessions in berlin hochschule für musik

philharmonisches orchester berlin

rossini il barbiere di siviglia overture

528 ½ gs 35028/91028/brunswick 95057/decca CA 8218
529 ½ gs

lp issues: heliodor 88 021/melodiya D 030275-030276

cd issues: symposium 1043/dante LYS 116/music and arts CD 954/ koch 3-7059-2/french furtwängler society SWF 042-044/naxos 8.111003/ andromeda ANDRCD 5008/japanese furtwängler society WFJ 15-16

weber der freischütz overture and act three entr'acte

542 1/2 gs 67108/566 177/brunswick 95030/decca CA 8262
543 1/2 gs
544gs 67109/566 178/brunswick 95031/decca CA 8263
545 3/4 gs

lp issues: rococo 2014/japan NA 121-122/deutsche grammophon 2535 821

cd issues: dante LYS 116/koch 3-7073-2/deutsche grammophon 459 0012 (overture only)/459 0652 (overture only)/membran 20.3090 (overture only)/20.3093 (overture only)/225 308 (overture only)/naxos 8.111004/ french furtwängler society SWF 042-044/andromeda ANDRCD 5008/ dutton CDVS 1920/japanese furtwängler society WFJ 22

entr'acte also published on polydor 95411; WFJ 22 also claims to contain alternative unpublished takes of the overture

The recommended CD version for the items in Session 019 remains French Furtwängler Society SWF 042-044

020/13, 15 and 18 october 1935/stage recordings in vienna staatsoper

chor und orchester der wiener staatsoper/anna bathy/ gotthelf pistor/georg maikl/ludwig hoffmann/alexander sved/franz markhoff/wilhelm wernigk/karl ettl

wagner tannhäuser: dich teure halle; gar viel und schön; vernehmt durch mich was gottes wille ist; dir hohe liebe töne; dir göttin der liebe; ein engel stieg aus lichtem äther; erbarm dich mein; als du in kühnem sange; wohl wusst ich hier; o du mein holder abendstern

unpublished authorised recordings: fragments of 3-5 minute duration taken down by hermann may on sheets of wax, gelatine or decelith

lp issues: unique opera recordings UORC 242/teletheater 643.333/ acanta 40.23520

cd issues: acanta 44.1055/koch 3-1470-2/istituto discografico italiano IDIS 330-331

most published editions make only a selection of the available items

021/9 january 1936/stage recordings in vienna staatsoper/

chor und orchester der wiener staatsoper/maria müller/ max lorenz

wagner tannhäuser: dir töne lob; dich teure halle; zu deinen füssen/ o stehet auf; seht mich die jungfrau/ich fleh für ihn; zum heil den sündigen zu führen/erbarm dich mein

unpublished authorised recordings: fragments of 3-5 minute duration taken down by hermann may on sheets of wax, gelatine or decelith

lp issue: teletheater 643.333

cd issues: koch 3-1470-2/istituto discografico italiano IDIS 330-331

most published editions make only a selection of the available items

022/13 and 17 february 1936/stage recordings in vienna staatsoper

orchester der wiener staatsoper/anny konetzni/maria müller/ rosette anday/franz völker/walter grossmann/alfred jerger/ luise helletsgruber/eva hadrabova/dora komarek/aenne michalsky/dora with/bella paalen/enid szantho

wagner die walküre: prelude; wes herd dies auch sei; labung biet ich; weither traun; auf den leichen lag sie tot; was gleisst dort hell?; hört mich an/eine waffe lass mich dir weisen; du bist der lenz; ein minnetraum; nun zäume dein ross/ hojotoho!; verweile süssestes weib; wo bist du siegmund?; nicht fahr ich nach walhall; walkürenritt; fort denn eile!/ o hehrstes wunder!; du zeugtest ein edles geschlecht; loge hör!; wer meines speeres spitze fürchtet

unpublished authorised recordings: fragments of 3-5 minute duration taken down by hermann may on sheets of wax, gelatine or decelith

lp issue: ed smith EJS 451/EJS 543

cd issues: koch 3-1470-2/dante LYS 217-218/istituto discografico italiano IDIS 330-331

most published editions make only a selection of the available items

The Wiener Staatsoper recordings in Sessions 021-022 initially demand some tolerance from the listener because of the restricted sound and the arbitrary breaks; however, particularly in the case of Die Walküre, we get a sense of occasion and the frisson of an actual performance, not to mention some Wagner singing of considerable stature

023 (042)/19 july 1936/stage recordings in bayreuth festspielhaus

chor und orchester der bayreuther festspiele/maria müller/ margarete klose/franz völker/josef von manowarda

wagner lohengrin: act three prelude; treulich geführt; das süsse lied verhallt; heil könig heinrich/habt dank ihr lieben von brabant; in fernem land; mein lieber schwan; fahr heim du stolzer helde...to end of act

unpublished acetates taken from the reichsrundfunk transmission

lp issues: ed smith EJS 399/cetra FE 25/french furtwängler society SWF 7801-7803/acanta HB 22 8630/40 23502/40 23520

cd issues: acanta 44 1055/fonoteam CD 94807/grammofono AB 78515/ iron needle IN 1634-1635/archipel ARPCD 0284/istituto discografico italiano IDIS 330-331/ venezia (japan) V 1024

some editions include opening radio announcement

Limited sound quality need not impair appreciation of this momentous occasion; the Archipel edition very conveniently couples the recordings with similar extracts recorded later in the Bayreuth season by Telefunken with the same soloists but conducted by Heinz Tietjen

024 (039 and 043)/28 december 1936/polydor sessions in berlin hochschule für musik

philharmonisches orchester berlin

mozart serenade no 13 in g K525 "eine kleine nachtmusik"

781 1/2 ge I 67156/67182/566 188/decca X 211
679 1/2 gs
680 1/2 gs 67157/67183/566 189/decca X 212
681 1/2 gs
785 1/2 ge 67158/67184/566 190/decca X 213
45rpm issue: deutsche grammophon EPL 30 576
lp issues: deutsche grammophon LPM 18 960/2535 827/2730 005/ melodiya D 030275-030276/heliodor (usa) H 25079/HS 25079
cd issues: dante LYS 117/deutsche grammophon 431 8732/477 5238/ koch 3-7079-2/membran 20.3090/20.3091/223 508/naxos 8.111136/ french furtwängler society SWF 042-044/andromeda ANDRCD 5008
sides 679, 680 and 681 were recorded in june 1937

johann strauss die fledermaus overture
786 1/2 ge 67121/91091/566 194
787 1/2 ge I
lp issues: heliodor 88 021/melodiya D 030275-030276/japan AT 09-10
cd issues: preiser 90090/membran 20.3090/20.3093/223 508/koch 3-7073-2/ naxos 8.111005/french furtwängler society SWF 042-044/ andromeda ANDRCD 5008

Naxos and French Furtwängler Society are the CD recommendations for the items in Session 024

025/1 may 1937/hmv concert recording in london queens hall/

philharmonisches orchester berlin/philharmonic choir of london/
erna berger/gertrud pitzinger/walther ludwig/rudolf watzke

beethoven symphony no 9 in d minor op 125 "choral"

2EA 3559 unpublished
2EA 3560
2EA 3561 unpublished
2EA 3562
2EA 3563 unpublished
2EA 3564
2EA 3565 unpublished
2EA 3566
2EA 3567 unpublished
2EA 3568
2EA 3569 unpublished
2EA 3570
2EA 3571 unpublished
2EA 3572
2EA 3573 unpublished
2EA 3574
2EA 3575 unpublished
2EA 3576
2EA 3577 unpublished

lp issues: emi ED 27 01231/toshiba WF 70073-70074

cd issues: toshiba TOCE 6067/dante LYS 073/music and arts CD 818/
emi 562 8752/japanese furtwängler society WFJ 19/japanese furtwängler centre WFFC 0301

these recordings were made over telephone lines from queens hall to abbey road studios and then transferred to 78rpm matrices; music and arts edition incorrectly described the chorus on this recording as bruno-kittel-chor

Olsen's 1973 discography mentioned an unidentified recording of the Ninth Symphony from April 1937: it is surmised that this London performance may be the same one

026/24 may 1937/hmv technical test series/stage recordings in london royal opera house

london philharmonic orchestra/rudolf bockelmann/kerstin thorborg/ josephine wray/edith furmedge/stella andreva/edith coates/henry wendon/erich zimmermann/paul schoeffler/eugen fuchs/ludwig weber/robert easton

wagner das rheingold

2EA 5201	unpublished
2EA 5202	
2EA 5203	unpublished
2EA 5204	
2EA 5205	unpublished
2EA 5206	
2EA 5207	unpublished
2EA 5208	
2EA 5209	unpublished
2EA 5210	
2EA 5211	unpublished
2EA 5212	
2EA 5213	unpublished
2EA 5214	
2EA 5215	unpublished
2EA 5216	
2EA 5217	unpublished
2EA 5218	
2EA 5219	unpublished
2EA 5220	
2EA 5221	unpublished
2EA 5222	
2EA 5223	unpublished
2EA 5224	
2EA 5225	unpublished
2EA 5226	
2EA 5227	unpublished
2EA 5228	

026/concluded

2EA 5229 unpublished
2EA 5230
2EA 5231 unpublished
2EA 5232
2EA 5233 unpublished
2EA 5234

027 (044)/26 may 1937/hmv technical test series/stage recordings in london royal opera house

london philharmonic orchestra/kirsten flagstad/maria müller/rudolf bockelmann/elsa stenning/mae craven/thelma bardsley/linda seymour/edith coates/evelyn arden/gwladys garside/gladys ripley

wagner die walküre: act three

2EA 5238 unpublished
2EA 5239
2EA 5240 unpublished
2EA 5241
2EA 5242 unpublished
2EA 5243
2EA 5244 unpublished
2EA 5245
2EA 5246 unpublished
2EA 5247
2EA 5248 unpublished
2EA 5249
2EA 5250 unpublished
2EA 5251
2EA 5252 unpublished
2EA 5253

lp issues: ed smith EJS 450/japan JPL 1020-1022/discocorp RR 417/acanta 40 23520
cd issues: acanta 44 1055/myto MCD 91443/grammofono AB 78512/
dante LYS 217-218/music and arts CD 1035

The quality of these recordings make it regrettable that publication of the entire Ring cycle still remains unlikely

028/28 may 1937/hmv technical test series/stage recordings in london royal opera house

london philharmonic orchestra/kirsten flagstad/edith furmedge/stella andreva/lauritz melchior/erich zimmermann/rudolf bockelmann/eugen fuchs/ robert easton

wagner siegfried; unspecified extracts

2EA 5609	unpublished
2EA 5610	
2EA 5611	unpublished
2EA 5612	
2EA 5613	unpublished
2EA 5614	
2EA 5615	unpublished
2EA 5616	
2EA 5617	unpublished
2EA 5618	

029 (045)/1 june 1937/hmv technical test series/stage recordings in london royal opera house

london philharmonic orchestra/royal opera chorus/kirsten flagstad/ kirstin thorborg/maria nezadal/lauritz melchior/herbert janssen/ ludwig weber/eugen fuchs/mary jarred/constance willis/mae craven/stella andreva/jose malone/linda seymour

wagner götterdämmerung: zu neuen taten; altgewohntes geräusch/to end of act one; heil dir gunther/to end of act two; her den ring/to end of act three

2EA 5619	unpublished
2EA 5620	
2EA 5621	unpublished
2EA 5622	
2EA 5623	unpublished
2EA 5624	
2EA 5625	unpublished
2EA 5626	
2EA 5627	unpublished
2EA 5628	
2EA 5629	unpublished
2EA 5630	
2EA 5631	unpublished
2EA 5632	
2EA 5633	unpublished
2EA 5634	
2EA 5635	unpublished
2EA 5636	
2EA 5637	unpublished
2EA 5638	
2EA 5639	unpublished
2EA 5640	
2EA 5641	unpublished
2EA 5642	

029/concluded

2EA 5643 unpublished
2EA 5644
2EA 5645 unpublished
2EA 5646

lp issues: ed smith EJS 431/japan JPL 1020-1022/discocorp RR 429
cd : eklipse EKR 62/dante LYS 219-221/music and arts CD 1035/
gebhardt JGCD 00032

030 (046)/8 october and 3 november 1937/electrola sessions in berlin philharmonie/*producer fred gaisberg*

philharmonisches orchester berlin

beethoven symphony no 5 in c minor op 67

2RA 2335 DB 3328/victor M 426
2RA 2336
2RA 2337 DB 3329/victor M 426
2RA 2338
2RA 2339 DB 3330/victor M 428
2RA 2340
2RA 2341 DB 3331/victor M 426
2RA 2342
2RA 2343 DB 3332/victor M 426

lp issues: emi 2C051 03587/3C 153 53800-53805M/
french furtwängler society SWF 7002
cd issues: novello NVLCD 904/music and arts CD 954/dante LYS 072/
membran 20.3090/20.3095/223 508/biddulph WHL 006/tahra FURT
1032-1033/naxos 8.110879/andromeda ANDRCD 5008/
japanese furtwängler society WFJ 15-16

78rpm edition also published in automatic coupling with numbers DB 8374-8378; japanese furtwängler society suggests that hmv and electrola used different takes of at least two of the 78rpm sides

The most vivid transfers of these records are to be found on the Biddulph and Naxos editions

031/25 november 1937/stage recordings in vienna staatsoper

chor und orchester der wiener staatsoper/maria reining/
enid szantho/max lorenz/erich zimmermann/karl kamann/
herbert alsen/hermann wiedemann/georg maikl/georg
monthy/fritz krenn/anton arnold/eduard fritsch/richard
tomek/walter hellmich/hermann reich/karl ettl

wagner die meistersinger von nürnberg: overture/da zu dir der heiland
kam; wann dann die flur vom frost befreit; fanget an!; jerum! jerum!;
den tag seh ich erscheinen; zu hilfe! zu hilfe!; act three prelude;
selig wie die sonne; jetzt all am fleck; silentium!; morgenlich leuchtend;
im drang der schlimmen jahr'

unpublished authorised recordings: fragments of 3-5 minute duration
taken down by hermann may on sheets of wax, gelatine or decelith

lp issue: teletheater 762 8691-762 8692

cd issue: koch 3-1470-2

lp edition contains only three of the fragments

032 (047 and 048)/11 february 1938/electrola sessions in berlin philharmonie/*producer walter michael berten*

philharmonisches orchester berlin

wagner tristan und isolde: vorspiel und liebestod

2RA 2657	DB 3419/victor M 653
2RA 2658	
2RA 2659	DB 3420/victor M 653
2RA 2660	

lp issues: hmv COLH 307/electrola SME 91399/unicorn WFS 2-3/
melodiya D 03367-03368/angel seraphim 6024/top classic TC 9054/
emi 2C061 00932/1C149 01197-01199M/F 666 701/bayreuth festival
1976

cd issues: dante LYS 115/music and arts CD 954/biddulph WHL 006/
membran 222 128/emi 764 9352/naxos 8.110865/andromeda
ANDRCD 5008

Best CD recommendation for these sessions is Biddulph or Naxos

033 (049 and 050)/15 march 1938/electrola sessions in berlin philharmonie/*producer walter michael berten*

philharmonisches orchester berlin

wagner parsifal prelude

2RA 2741 DB 3445/victor M 514

2RA 2742

2RA 2743 DB 3446/victor M 514

wagner parsifal: karfreitagszauber

2RA 2744 DB 3446/victor M 514

2RA 2745 DB 3447/victor M 514

2RA 2746

lp issues: hmv COLH 307/electrola SME 91399/SMVP 8055-8056/ unicorn WFS 2-3/angel seraphim 6024/top classic TC 9054/emi RLS 768 (karfreitagszauber)/29 12343/1C147 29229-29230/ 1C149 01197-01199M/acanta 40 23520 (prelude)/ discocorp RR 229 (prelude)

cd issues: acanta 43 121 (prelude)/44 1055 (prelude)/membran 20.3090/ 20.3092/223 508/magic talent MT 48090 (prelude)/grammofono AB 78515 (prelude)/dante LYS 115/iron needle IN 1364-1365 (prelude)/ biddulph WHL 006/emi 764 9352/naxos 8.110879/andromeda ANDRCD 5008/archipel ARPCD 0261

78rpm edition also published in automatic coupling with the numbers DB 8494-8496

Best CD recommendation for these sessions is Biddulph or Naxos

034 (051)/1 june 1938/stage recording in london royal opera house

london philharmonic orchestra/frida leider/kerstin thorborg/ karl kamann

wagner die walküre: hojotoho!/des frech frevelnden paars

lp issues: unique opera recordings UORC 234/ed smith EJS 170/EJS 234

cd issue: frida-leider-gesellschaft FLG 193 61938

035 (052)/7 june 1938/stage recordings in london royal opera house

london philharmonic orchestra/royal opera chorus/frida leider/
anny von stosch/lauritz melchior/herbert janssen/wilhelm schirp

wagner götterdämmerung: heil dir gunther to end of act two

lp issue: ed smith EJS 342/acanta 40 23502

cd issues: eklipse EKR 62/dante LYS 219-221/pearl GEMMCD 9331/gebhardt JGCD 00032/frida-leider-gesellschaft FLG 193 61938

A performance of almost painful tension, which would be essential in any Wagner collection regardless of sound quality

036 (053)/5 september 1938/stage recordings in nürnberg opernhaus

chor und orchester der wiener staatsoper/chor des nürnberger opernhauses/tiana lemnitz/rut berglund/eyvind laholm/
erich zimmermann/rudolf bockelmann/eugen fuchs/
josef von manowarda/ julius katona/erich bürger/georg hann/
georg heckel/karl mikorey/julius brombacher/wolfgang markgraf/
andre von diehl/hans krenn

wagner die meistersinger von nürnberg: overture/da zu dir der heiland kam; halt meister nicht so geeilt!; was duftet doch der flieder/guten abend meister; jerum jerum!; wollt mich beim wahne fangen; so lang es beckmesser lebt; ist das erlaubt so spät zur nacht?; act three prelude; wahn wahn überall wahn!/ grüss gott mein junker; doch lass dem ruh/mein freund in holder jugendzeit; o sachs mein freund!/da streicht die lene schon ums haus/ein kind ward hier geboren; selig wie die sonne; wach auf!; sein töchterlein sein höchstes gut; das lied fürwahr ist nicht von mir; verachtet mir die meister nicht/ ehrt eure deutschen meister!

lp issues: unique opera recordings UORC 224/japan JP 1143-1144/ acanta 40 23520

cd issues: acanta 44 1055/koch 3-1452-2/grammofono AB 78610/iron needle IN 1364-1365/walhall WLCD 0050

this was a guest performance by the vienna staatsoper; not all editions contains all the material listed

The Koch CD issue is recommended for completeness and best sound

037 (054)/25-27 october 1938/electrola sessions in berlin philharmonie/*producer walter michael berten*

philharmonisches orchester berlin

tchaikovsky symphony no 6 in b minor op 64 "pathetique"

2RA 3345	DB 4609/victor M 553
2RA 3346	
2RA 3347	DB 4610/victor M 553
2RA 3348	
2RA 3349	DB 4611/victor M 553
2RA 3353	
2RA 3354	DB 4612/victor M 553
2RA 3355	
2RA 3356	DB 4613/victor M 553
2RA 3350	
2RA 3351	DB 4614/victor M 553
2RA 3352	

lp issues: hmv COLH 21/TRX 6140/electrola E 91079/world records H 107/ emi RLS 768/F669.711-669.715/melodiya D 020049-020050

cd issues: novello NVLCD 904/claremont GSE 78 5051/palladio PD 4122/ historical performers HP 14/grammofono AB 78558/membran 20.3090/ 20.3091/223 508/music and arts CD 954/emi 764 8552/300 0122/907 8782/ biddulph WHL 007/naxos 8.110865/andromeda ANDRCD 5008/dutton CDVS 1920/tahra FURT 1099-1100/japanese furtwängler society WFJS 15-16

78rpm edition was also published in automatic coupling with numbers DB 8600-8605

Fred Gaisberg, who was also present at the sessions, noted in an internal memorandum "We compliment everyone concerned in the production of these magnificent records". Personally I can clearly recall the devastating effect the LP transfer on COLH 21 had on me: if pressed to make a CD choice, I would opt for Biddulph or Naxos

038 (055)/19 january 1939/reichsrundfunk recording in berlin philharmonie

philharmonisches orchester berlin/edwin fischer (piano)

furtwängler symphonic concerto in b minor for piano and orchestra

EA 50570	unpublished
EA 50571	
EA 50572	unpublished
EA 50573	
EA 50574	unpublished
EA 50575	
EA 50576	unpublished
EA 50577	
EA 50578	unpublished
EA 50579	
EA 50580	unpublished
EA 50581	
EA 50582	unpublished
EA 50583	
EA 50584	unpublished
EA 50585	
EA 50586	unpublished
EA 50587	

cd issues: pilz CD 78004/dante LYS 123

039 (056)/25 april 1939/electrola session in berlin philharmonie

philharmonisches orchester berlin/edwin fischer (piano)

furtwängler symphonic concerto in b minor for piano and orchestra:
second movement

2RA 3904	DB 4696
2RA 3905	
2RA 3906	DB 4697

lp issues: french furtwängler society SWF 7101/japan JP 1101-1102/
emi HLM 7027/1C047 01415M/discocorp MLG 74

cd issues: music and arts CD 954/membran 20.3090/20.3093/223 508/
biddulph WHL 007/testament SBT 1170/naxos 8.110879/
andromeda ANDRCD 5008/emi 907 878

040/13 september 1939/reichsrundfunk recordings in berlin philharmonie/*sound engineer friedrich schnapp*

philharmonisches orchester berlin

handel concerto grosso in d op 6 no 5

EA 55966 unpublished
EA 55967
EA 55968 unpublished
EA 55969
EA 55970 unpublished
cd issues: tahra FURT 1014-1015/membran 20.3090/20.3093/
223 508

beethoven symphony no 5 in c minor op 67

EA 55971 unpublished
EA 55972
EA 55973 unpublished
EA 55974
EA 55975 unpublished
EA 55976
EA 55977 unpublished
EA 55978
EA 55979 unpublished
EA 55980
cd issue: tahra FURT 1014-1015

matrix EA 55979 being missing from the source, it is replaced by tahra with the same section from the 1937 hmv recording (session 030)

According to Rene Tremine this session was the first of a series arranged by the National Socialists with Reichsrundfunk, whereby works being played in concurrent Philharmonic Concerts would be preserved for broadcast later

041 (059)/15 october 1940/telefunken session in berlin philharmonie

philharmonisches orchester berlin

beethoven cavatina from string quartet in b flat op 130, arranged for string orchestra

025238 SK 3104

025239

45rpm issue: telefunken LV 115

lp issues: telefunken LS 6025/capitol H 8130/rococo 2013/japan JP 1101-1102/AT 07-08/french furtwängler society SWF 7702

cd issues: french furtwängler society SWF 901/teldec 9031 764352/ music and arts CD 954/tahra FURT 1012-1013/andromeda ANDRCD 5008/naxos 8.110095

My view is that no CD transfer of this performance has equalled the natural ambience of the LP from French Furtwängler Society

042 (060)/21-22 december 1940/concert recording in vienna musikvereinssaal

wiener philharmoniker/wilhelm furtwängler (piano)/ wolfgang schneiderhan (violin)/josef niedermayer (flute)

bach brandenburg concerto no 5 in d BWV 1050

lp issues: french furtwängler society SWF 8401-8402/japan AT 13-14

043 (061)/2-4 february 1941/concert recording in berlin philharmonie/*sound engineer friedrich schnapp*

philharmonisches orchester berlin

bruckner symphony no 7 in e

lp issue: japan AT 11-12

This recording is transferred from acetates and sadly has many gaps in the music, with the finale missing entirely

044 (064)/14-16 december 1941/concert recording in berlin philharmonie/*sound engineer friedrich schnapp*

philharmonisches orchester berlin

bruckner symphony no 4 in e flat "romantic"

lp issue: japan AT 11-12

cd issues: delta (japan) DCCA 0001/japanese furtwängler centre WFHC 018-020

This recording is transferred from acetates and sadly has many gaps in the music

045 (065)/25 december 1941/stage recordings in vienna staatsoper

orchester der wiener staatsoper/anni konetzni/margarete klose/max lorenz

wagner tristan und isolde: hörst du sie nach?; frau minne kenntest du nicht?; sink hernieder nacht der liebe; selbst dann bin ich der welt/ einsam wachend; so stürben wir; wohin nun tristan scheidet

unpublished authorised recordings: fragments of 3-5 minutes duration taken by hermann may on sheets of wax, gelatine or decelith

lp issues: unique opera recordings UORC 267/ed smith EJS 399/ acanta 22 863

cd issues: koch 3-1456-2/3-1461-2/radio years RY 76

some editions make only a selection of the available items

046 (066)/7 january 1942/stage recording in vienna staatsoper

chor und orchester der wiener staatsoper/hans hotter

beethoven fidelio: ha welch ein augenblick!

lp issue: unique opera recordings UORC 242

It is not clear if this extract is from the Hermann May source

047/15-17 february 1942/concert recordings in berlin philharmonie/*sound engineer friedrich schnapp*

philharmonisches orchester berlin/peter anders

strauss don juan
discocorp RR 476
cd issues: deutsche grammophon 427 7822/427 7732/471 2942/russian compact disc RCD 25008/melodiyaMEL 10 00717/music and arts CD 829/ membran 20.3090/20.3093/223 508/chibas restorations 1120/french furtwängler society SWF 031-032

strauss orchesterlieder: waldseligkeit; liebeshymnus; verführung; winterliebe
lp issues: melodiya M10 41233-41234/french furtwängler society SWF 7906/ discocorp IGI 382/nippon columbia OZ 7603/arabesque AR 8082/cetra FE 41
cd issues: priceless D 18355/arabesque Z 6082/melodiya M10 00723/ russian compact disc RCD 25014/dante LYS 203/music and arts CD 829/ tahra FURT 201-202/FURT 1038-1039/chibas restorations 1110

These Reichsrundfunk recordings can be best heard on the Russian Compact Disc or Chibas Restorations issues

048/26 february 1942/newsreel soundtrack recording in berlin aeg factory (werkkonzert)

philharmonisches orchester berlin

wagner die meistersinger von nürnberg overture
lp issues: french furtwängler society SWF 8801-8803/japan AT 09-10/W 22-23
cd issue: tahra FURT 1036-1037/chibas restorations 1121-1124/ archipel ARPCD 0261
vhs video: bel canto society BCS 0052
dvd video: arthaus 101 453

Although the performance can be seen (either complete or in excerpt) in various film documentaries about Furtwängler, the most vivid sound is to be experienced from the French Furtwängler Society LP or Chibas Restorations editions

049 (067)/1-3 march 1942/concert recording in berlin philharmonie/*sound engineer friedrich schnapp*

philharmonisches orchester berlin/walter gieseking (piano)

schumann piano concerto in a minor op 54

lp issues: melodiya M10 36605-36606/everest SDBR 8434/discocorp IGI 348/nippon columbia OZ 7596/french furtwängler society SWF 7701

cd issues: melodiya MEL 10 00719/russian compact disc RCD 25010/ deutsche grammophon 427 7792/427 7732/471 2942/dante LYS 196/ arlecchino ARL 151-152/opus kura OPK 7012/chibas restorations 1119/ pristine audio PASC 347

050 (068)/22-24 march 1942/concert recording in berlin philharmonie/*sound engineer friedrich schnapp*

philharmonisches orchester berlin/bruno-kittel-chor/tilla briem/ elisabeth höngen/peter anders/rudolf watzke

beethoven symphony no 9 in d minor op 125 "choral"

lp issues: melodiya D 010851-010854/M10 10851 009/unicorn UNI 100-101/vox turnabout TV 4346-4347/TV 4353-4354/french furtwängler society SWF 7003-7004/nippon columbia DXM 105-106/ everest SDBR 3241/emi 3C153 53810-53816M

cd issues: priceless D 13256/french furtwängler society SWF 891/ music and arts CD 653/arkadia CDWFE 357/melodiya MEL 10 00715/ russian compact disc RCD 25006/documents LV 919-920/historical performers HP 6/grammofono AB 78581/dante LYS 071/tahra FURT 1004-1007/FURT 1036-1037/opus kura OPK 7003/chibas restorations 1106

This iconic performance has received numerous transfers since the original Melodiya LPs, the most successsful perhaps being those by Tahra; however, those collectors familiar with the recording throughout its published history will probably been drawn to those CD transfers (Melodiya and Russian Compact Disc) which retain the roughness, almost danger, of the early LP editions

051 (069)/7 april 1942/telefunken session in berlin philharmonie

philharmonisches orchester berlin

bruckner symphony no 7: second movement

026378 SK 3230/ultraphon 922264

026379

026380 SK 3231/ultraphon 922265

026381

026382 SK 3232/ultraphon 922266

026383

lp issues: rococo 2014/japan JP 1101-1102/AT 11-12/discocorp RR 457/ french furtwängler society SWF 7702/SWF 8801-8802

cd issues: teldec 9031 764352/french furtwängler society SWF 963/dante LYS 106-107/music and arts CD 954/tahra FURT 1004-1007/naxos 8.111000/ tahra FURT 1099-1100/andromeda ANDRCD 5008/chibas restorations 1114/ japanese furtwängler society WFJ 17

French Furtwängler Society LP transfer would be hard to improve upon, but for a CD choice one might turn to Naxos or Chibas Restorations

052/19 april 1942/concert recording in berlin philharmonie

philharmonisches orchester berlin/bruno-kittel-chor/erna berger/ gertrud pitzinger/helge rosvaenge/rudolf watzke

beethoven symphony no 9 in d minor op 125 "choral"

cd issue: archipel ARPCD 0270

Recorded privately from radio broadcast onto 78rpm decelith discs, this was the occasion on which Furtwängler was manoeuvred into conducting for Adolf Hitler's official birthday celebration; the final bars and concluding applause were also filmed for Deutsche Wochenschau and can be seen in various film documentaries about the conductor (but with the sound taken from the 22-24 March performance (Session no. 050))

053/21-24 april 1942/concert recording in vienna musikvereinssaal

wiener philharmoniker

beethoven symphony no 9: third movement

cd issue: symposium 1253

Like the performance of the Ninth Symphony a few days earlier in Berlin, this recording was also made privately onto 78rpm decelith discs

054 (071)/25-28 october 1942/concert recordings in berlin philharmonie/*sound engineer friedrich schnapp*

philharmonisches orchester berlin/tibor de machula (cello)

schumann cello concerto

lp issues: melodiya M10 42555-42558/french furtwängler society SWF 8201-8202/discocorp RR 538/nippon columbia OZ 7596

cd issues: melodiya MEL 10 00721/russian compact disc RCD 25012/ dante LYS 196/deutsche grammophon 427 7792/427 7732/471 2942/ arlecchino ARL 151-152/chibas restorations

bruckner symphony no 5 in b flat

lp issues: melodiya M10 42555-42558/french furtwängler society SWF 8203-8204/discocorp RR 538/nippon columbia OZ 7600

cd issues: bella musica BMF 967/melodiya MEL 10 00714/russian compact disc RCD 25005/deutsche grammophon 427 7742/427 7732/ 471 2942/dante LYS 108/music and arts CD 538/german furtwängler society WFG 2011/opus kura OPK 7013/chibas restorations 1113

The two works from this Philharmonic Concert can be heard most favourably on the issue from Chibas Restorations

055 (072)/29 october 1942/telefunken session in berlin singakademie

philharmonisches orchester berlin

gluck alceste overture

029753 SK 3266/T 122/GX 61008/capitol 81001

029754

45rpm issue: telefunken UV 115

lp issues: telefunken LS 6025/capitol H 8130/japan JP 1101-1102/
AT 09-10/french furtwängler society SWF 7702/melodiya M10 46683 000

cd issues: melodiya MEL 10 00724/russian compact disc RCD 25015/
dante LYS 117/membran 20.3090/20.3093/223 508/music and arts CD 954/
teldec 9031 764352/naxos 8.110994/andromeda ANDRCD 5008/
chibas restorations 1117

056 (073)/8-9 november 1942/concert recordings in berlin philharmonie/_sound engineer friedrich schnapp_

philharmonisches orchester berlin/edwin fischer (piano)

brahms piano concerto no 2 in b flat op 83

lp: melodiya D 09883-09884/unicorn UNI 102/french furtwängler society
SWF 6901/nippon columbia DXM 108/emi 1C149 53420-53426/29 09701/
2C153 53420-53426/3C153 53661-53669M

cd issues: deutsche grammophon 427 7782/427 7732/471 2942/priceless
D 14236/melodiya MEL 10 00724/russian compact disc RCD 25015/
music and arts CD 804/dante LYS 046/testament SBT 1170/venezia V-1002/
opus kura OPK 7018/chibas restorations 1110/pristine audio PASC 347

wagner tristan und isolde: vorspiel und liebestod

lp issues: melodiya M10 45949 008/french furtwängler society
SWF 8801-8803

cd issues: melodiya MEL 10 00721/russian compact disc RCD 25012/
music and arts CD 730/tahra FURT 1004-1007/FURT 1036-1037/
archipel ARPCD 0261/chibas restorations 1121-1124

057 (074-076)/25 november 1942/concert recordings in stockholm konserthuset

stockholms konsertförenings orkester

strauss don juan

lp issues: orfeus (sweden) 1-73-2/nippon columbia OZ 7512/ french furtwängler society SWF 8403-8404

cd issue: music and arts CD 814

wagner tristan und isolde: vorspiel und liebestod

lp issue: music and arts RR 505

cd issues: bis BISCD 424B/membran 20.3090/29.3092/223 508/ grammofono AB 78515/music and arts CD 794

058 (070)/6-8 december 1942/concert recordings in berlin philharmonie/*sound engineer friedrich schnapp*

philharmonisches orchester berlin/erna berger/ walther ludwig/fritz heitmann (organ)

heinz schubert hymnisches konzert für sopran, tenor, orgel u.orchester

lp issue: melodiya M10 49723 000

cd issues: melodiya MEL 10 00725/russian compact disc RCD 25016/ grammofono AB 78510/arkadia CDWFE 365

schubert symphony no 9 in c D944 "great"

lp issues: melodiya D 010033-010034/M10 10033 007/turnabout TV 4364/ nippon columbia DXM 109/french furtwängler society SWF 7201

cd issues: priceless D 13272/bayer da capo 20 003/melodiya MEL 10 00723/ russian compact disc RCD 25014/deutsche grammophon 427 7812/427 7732/ 471 2892/palladio PD 4176/dante LYS 114/music and arts CD 826/german furtwängler society TMK 017204/french furtwängler society SWF 031-032/ japanese furtwängler society/opus kura OPK 7010/chibas restorations 1118/ pristine audio PASC 253

This version of the Schubert Great C major being much rougher hewn than Furtwängler's 1951 recording for DG , there is perhaps an argument for the more primitive and edgy sonics of the original issues; however, Chibas Restorations give us a cleaner sound

059 (078)/2 january 1943/stage recordings in vienna staatsoper

chor und orchester der wiener staatsoper/anni konetzni/
margarete klose/max lorenz/paul schoeffler/herbert alsen/
georg monthy/karl ettl/willy franter/hermann gallos

wagner tristan und isolde: westwärts schweift der blick; auf jeder stelle
wo ich steh; auf das tau! anker los!; tristan! isolde! trauteste holde!;
act three complete but without prelude

cd issue: koch 3-1461-2

Koch gives us here by far the most important of the Hermann May recordings as far as Wilhelm Furtwängler is concerned, with a virtually unbroken sequence from Act Three; this was also the occasion on which, as well as conducting, Furtwängler also took responsibility for stage direction

060 (079)/7-8 february 1943/concert recordings in berlin philharmonie/*sound engineer friedrich schnapp*

philharmonisches orchester berlin/georg kulenkampff (violin)

sibelius violin concerto in d minor op 47

lp issues: melodiya M10 45909 004/nippon columbia DXM 112/
french furtwängler society SWF 8604/unicorn UNI 107

cd issues: melodiya MEL 10 00718/russian compact disc RCD 25009/
music and arts CD 799/archipel ARPCD 0014/chibas restorations 1125

sibelius en saga

lp issues: melodiya M10 45909 004/french furtwängler society SWF 8604

cd issues: melodiya MEL 10 00718/russian compact disc RCD 25009/
deutsche grammophon 427 7832/427 7732/471 2942/grammofono AB 78558/
music and arts CD 799/french furtwängler society SWF 031-032/
chibas restorations 1125

Chibas Restorations is probably the best recommendation for these sole surviving examples of Furtwängler as a Sibelius interpreter

061 (80-82)/12 may 1943/concert recordings in stockholm konserthuset

wiener philharmoniker

schubert symphony no 8 in b minor "unfinished": first movement
lp issues: french furtwängler society SWF 8403-8404/japan AT 05-06
cd issues: french furtwängler society SWF 973/dante LYS 109/ music and arts CD 802/chibas restorations 1139

symphony no 9 in c D944 "great"
lp issues: discocorp RR 405/japan JP 1190-1192/nippon columbia OZ 7589/french furtwängler society SWF 8403-8404
cd issues: french furtwängler society SWF 973/membran 20.3090/ 20.3093/223 508/music and arts CD 802/chibas restorations 1139

johann strauss kaiserwalzer: incomplete recording
lp issue: french furtwängler society SWF 8403-8404
cd issues: french furtwängler society SWF 973/music and arts CD 802

062 (083)/27-30 june 1943/concert recording in berlin philharmonie (first performance)/*sound engineer friedrich schnapp*

philharmonisches orcheser berlin

beethoven symphony no 4 in b flat op 60
lp issues: melodiya D 09083-09084/vox PL 7210/olympic OL 8120/ OL 8124/nippon columbia DXM 103/deutsche grammophon LPM 18 742/2535 813/2730 005/eterna 820 312/vox turnabout TV 4344/french furtwängler society SWF 7103/emi 3C153 53810-53816M
cd issues: melodiya MEL 10 00719/russian compact disc RCD 25010/ deutsche grammophon 427 7772/427 7732/471 2892/grammofono AB 78502/dante LYS 072/music and arts CD 824/french furtwängler society SWF 011-013/opus kura OPK 7002/chibas restorations 1102

All LP editions of this recording contained only the first and second movements, to which were added the third and fourth movements from the Reichsrundfunk recording without audience (Session No. 064)

063/27-30 june 1943/concert recording in berlin philharmonie (second performance)/*sound engineer friedrich schnapp*

philharmonisches orchester berlin

beethoven symphony no 4: first and second movements

lp issue: french furtwängler society SWF 8801-8803

cd issues: french furtwängler society SWF 011-013/venezia V-1022/ chibas restorations 1102

despite the claims of french furtwänglersociety, it is felt that this is an identical recording to that in session no. 062

064 (084)/27-30 june 1943/reichsrundfunk recording in berlin philharmonie (without audience)/

sound engineer friedrich schnapp

philharmonisches orchester berlin

beethoven symphony no 4 in b flat op 60

lp issues: vox PL 7210/vox turnabout TV 4344/eterna 820 312/ deutsche grammophon LPM 18 742/2535 813/2730 005/ french furtwängler society SWF 7103

cd issue: french furtwängler society SWF 011-013/opus kura OPK 7017/ chibas restorations 1103

It should be noted that the LP editions of this recording contained only the third and fourth movements, to which were added the first and second movements from the concert recording with audience (Sesssion No. 062)

065 (085-086)/27-30 june 1943/concert recordings in berlin philharmonie/*sound engineer friedrich schnapp*

philharmonisches orchester berlin

beethoven symphony no 5 in c minor op 67
lp issues: melodiya D05800-05801/M10 05800 009/unicorn UNI 106/
nippon columbia DXM 157/ french furtwängler society SWF 7002/
vox turnabout TV 4353/TV 4361/TV 34478/ariston ARCL 13029/
emi 3C153 53810-53816M
cd issues: deutsche grammophon 427 7752/427 7732/471 2892/
melodiya MEL 10 00720/russian compact disc RCD 25011/grammofono
AB 78502/music and arts CD 824/dante LYS 065/tahra FURT 272/
FURT 1034-1035/ FURT 1032-1033/emi 562 8752/opus kura OPK 7001/
chibas restorations 1102/venezia V-1021
emi 562 8752 is incorrectly dated 7 february 1944

beethoven coriolan overture op 62
lp issues: melodiya D 09867-09868/M10 09867 006/discocorp SID 713/
nippon columbia DXM 103/french furtwängler society SWF 7002/
emi 3C153 53810-53816M
cd issues: deutsche grammophon 427 7802/427 7732/453 8042/
453 7002/471 2892/melodiya MEL 10 00718/russian compact disc
RCD 25009/membran 20.3090/20.3095/223 508/grammofono
AB 78502/dante LYS 064/music and arts CD 826/CD 942/tahra
FURT 1004-1007/chibas restorations 1103/ german furtwängler
society TMK 017204/japanese furtwängler society WFJ 23/
opus kura OPK 7026/venezia V-1024
concluding pizzicato chords were missing on original reichsrundfunk tape but have been restored electronically on many later editions

066 (087)/15 july 1943/stage recording in bayreuth festspielhaus

chor und orchester der bayreuther festspiele/maria müller/ camilla kallub/max lorenz/erich zimmermann/jaro prohaska/ eugen fuchs/josef greindl/fritz krenn/benno arnold/helmut fehn/gerhard witting/gustav rödin/karl krollmann/herbert gosebruch/franz sauer/alfred dome/erich pina

wagner die meistersinger von nürnberg

lp issues: unique opera recordings UORC 266/estro armonico EA 008/ foyer FO 1043/emi 1C181 01797-01801M

cd issues: laudis LCD 44008/dante LYS 026-029/grammofono AB 78602-78605/french furtwängler society SWF 081-084/ walhall WLCD 0050/chibas restorations 1121-1124

The mystery as to why opening scene of the opera as well as the crucial Act Three Quintet are missing remains unexplained: French Furtwängler Society and Chibas have carried out a remarkable restoration of the original tapes, but it is also noted that Walhall includes in its edition the Meistersinger extracts from Nürnberg in 1938 (Session No. 036)

067 (088-089)/31 october-3 november 1943/concert recordings in berlin philharmonie/*sound engineer friedrich schnapp*

philharmonisches orchester berlin/conrad hansen (piano)

ernst pepping symphony no 2 in f minor
lp issues: melodiya M10 049721 000/japan AT 13-14
cd issues: melodiya MEL 10 00725/russian compact disc RCD 25016/ arkadia CDWFE 365/grammofono AB 78510

beethoven piano concerto no 4 in g op 58
lp issues: unicorn UNI 106/french furtwängler society SWF 7005R/ nippon columbia DXM 104/deutsche grammophon 2535 807/emi 3C153 53010-53016M/melodiya M10 46067 003
cd issues: melodiya MEL 10 00771/russian compact discs RCD 25002/ french furtwängler society SWF 941/SWF 941R/arkadia CDWFE 365/ music and arts CD 839/tahra FURT 1034-1035/chibas restorations 1101/ dreamlife DCLA 7007

beethoven symphony no 7 in a op 92
lp issues: melodiya D 027779-027780/vox turnabout TV 34509/ unicorn WFS 8/french furtwängler society SWF 7105/olympic OL 8120/OL 8129/intercord 120 924/emi 3C153 53810-53816M
cd issues: deutsche grammophon 427 7752/427 7732/471 2892/ melodiya MEL 10 00713/russian compact disc RCD 25004/french furtwängler society SWF 941/SWF 941R/opus kura OPK 7002/ chibas restorations 1104/dreamlife DCLA 7007

Both French Furtwängler Society and Chibas Restorations have produced exemplary editions of the Beethoven works from this concert

068 (090)/13-16 november 1943/concert recordings in berlin philharmonie/*sound engineer friedrich schnapp*

philharmonisches orchester berlin/pierre fournier (cello)

bruckner symphony no 6 in a

lp issues: melodiya M10 47465 005/japan W 28-29/
french furtwängler society SWF 8801-8803

cd issues: melodiya MEL 10 00720/russian compact disc RCD 25011/
dante LYS 106-107/music and arts CD 805/french furtwängler society
SWF 963/emi 566 2102/tahra FURT 1004-1007/chibas restorations 1114

first movement of the symphony is unfortunately missing from source

schumann cello concerto

cd issues: tahra FURT 1008-1011/dante LYS 196/venezia (japan) V 1002/
chibas restorations 1119/japanese furtwängler society WFJ 23

first and second movements unfortunately missing from source

strauss till eulenspiegels lustige streiche

45rpm issues: deutsche grammophon EPL 30 589/eterna 520 439

lp issues: deutsche grammophon LPM 18 960/2535 816/2548 719/
2721 202/royale 1259/1370/gramophone (usa) 2097

cd issues: deutsche grammophon 427 7832/427 7732/439 8372/
471 2942/music and arts CD 829/chibas restorations 1120/french
furtwängler society SWF 031-032

royale and gramophone editions did not identify conductor;
deutsche grammophon editions LPM 18 960 and 2548 719
were both incorrectly dated

069 (091)/8 december 1943/concert recording in stockholm konserthuset

stockholms konsertförenings orkester/musikaliska sällskapets kör/ hjördis schymberg/lisa tunell/gösta bäckelin/sigurd björling

beethoven symphony no 9 in d minor op 125
lp issues: olympic OL 8120/japan JP 1119-1120/discocorp RR 206
cd issues: dante LYS 066/music and arts WFSA 2002/CD 2002/tahra TAH 488-489

070 (092-094)/12-15 december 1943/concert recordings in berlin philharmonie/*sound engineer friedrich schnapp*

philharmonisches orchester berlin/adrian aeschbacher (piano)

brahms haydn variations op 56a
lp issues: melodiya D 010851-010854/M10 10851 009/unicorn UNI 100-101/ everest SDBR 3252/nippon columbia DXM 104/OS 7076/french furtwängler society SWF 8203-8204/emi 3C153 53661-53669M
cd issues: priceless D 14236/melodiya MEL 10 00722/russian compact disc RCD 25013/magic talent MT 48059/grammofono AB 78594/dante LYS 049/ music and arts CD 805/ CD 941/tahra FURT 1038-1039/opus kura OPK 7010/ chibas restorations 1112

brahms piano concerto no 2 in b flat op 83
lp issues: melodiya M10 45921 009/french furtwängler society SWF 8502
cd issues: french furtwängler society SWF 951-952/music and arts CD 941/ dante LYS 049/tahra FURT 1004-1007/FURT 1038-1039/chibas restorations 1109

brahms symphony no 4 in e minor op 98
lp issues: melodiya D 09867-09868/M10 09867 006/rococo 2013/nippon columbia DXM 107/OW 7823/discocorp RR 418/emi 3C153 53661-53669M
cd issues: melodiya MEL 10 00722/russian compact disc RCD 25013/magic talent MT 48059/arkadia CDWFE 365/french furtwängler society SWF 951-952/ grammofono AB 78594/dante LYS 048/music and arts CD 804/CD 941/ tahra FURT 1038-1039/chibas restorations 1112/venezia V-1024/ opus kura OPK 7012/pristine audio PASC 344

This entire Brahms concert can be experienced as an entity on both Music and Arts CD 941 and Chibas Restorations

071 (095-096)/18-23 december 1943/electrola sessions in vienna musikvereinssaal

wiener philharmoniker

brahms haydn variations op 56a

2RA 6028 unpublished
2RA 6029
2RA 6030 unpublished
2RA 6031
2RA 6032 unpublished
2RA 6033

lp issues: french furtwängler society SWF 7602/discocorp RR 456/emi ED 29 06661
cd issues: music and arts CD 804/CD 954/dante LYS 046-047/preiser 90199/
tahra FURT 1012-1013/chibas restorations 1108/french furtwängler society SWF 091
SWF 7602 and FURT 1012-1013 also include a selection of unapproved takes of individual variations; CD 804 incorrectly described as berlin 1943

beethoven symphony no 6 in f op 68 "pastoral"

2RA 6038 unpublished
2RA 6039
2RA 6040 unpublished
2RA 6041
2RA 6042 unpublished
2RA 6043
2RA 6045 unpublished
2RA 6046
2RA 6047 unpublished
2RA 6048
2RA 6049 unpublished

lp issues: vox turnabout TV 4408/nippon columbia DXM 131/emi ED 29 06661
cd issues: music and arts CD 954/dante LYS 074/preiser 90199/
chibas restorations 1108/french furtwängler society SWF 091
emi edition included a first movement repeat which was not sanctioned by the conductor

The Preiser edition is recommended for both the works in this session

072/9-12 january 1944/concert recordings in berlin philharmonie/*sound engineer friedrich schnapp*

philharmonisches orchester berlin/erich röhn (violin)

beethoven violin concerto in d op 61

lp issues: melodiya M10 40929-40930/french furtwängler society SWF 7901/discocorp IGI 364

cd issues: melodiya MEL 10 00716/russian compact disc RCD 25007/ as-disc AS 331-332/membran 20.3090/20.3095/223 508/deutsche grammophon 427 7802/427 7732/471 2892/french furtwängler society SWF 011-013/opus kura OPK 7017/chibas restorations 1101

strauss sinfonia domestica

lp issues: melodiya M10 40961-40962/french furtwängler society SWF 7902/discocorp IGI 364/arabesque AR 8082/cetra FE 41

cd issues: arabesque Z 6082/as-disc AS 331-332/melodiya MEL 10 00717/russian compact disc RCD 25008/deutsche grammophon 427 7822/427 7732/471 2942/ dante LYS 203/magic talent MT 48090/arlecchino ARL 111-112/chibas restorations 1120

This final concert in the Old Philharmonie before its destruction by Allied bombs was captured in excellent sound: probably the best transfer is that by Chibas Restorations

073/7-8 february 1944/concert recordings in berlin staatsoper unter den linden/*sound engineer friedrich schnapp*

philharmonisches orchester berlin

mozart symphony no 39 in e flat K543
lp issues: melodiya M10 46005 000/french furtwängler society SWF 8601
cd issues: melodiya MEL 10 00716/russian compact disc RCD 25007/ dante LYS 117/iron needle IN 1340/deutsche grammophon 427 7762/ 427 7732/471 2892/chibas restorations 1117

handel concerto grosso in d minor op 6 no 10
lp issues: melodiya M10 46005 000/french furtwängler society SWF 8601
cd issues: melodiya MEL 10 00721/russian compact disc RCD 25012/dante LYS 250/ deutsche grammophon 427 7772/427 7732/471 2892/ chibas restorations 1117

Deutsche Grammophon is the best recommendation for this coupling

074 (099)/20-21 march 1944/concert recordings in berlin staatsoper unter den linden/*sound engineer friedrich schnapp*

philharmonisches orchester berlin

weber der freischütz overture

lp issues: melodiya M10 41233-41234/french furtwängler society SWF 8203-8204/japan AT 09-10

cd issues: deutsche grammophon 427 7812/427 7732/471 2892/ melodiya MEL 10 00712/russian compact disc RCD 25003/music and arts CD 826/chibas restorations 1117/french furtwängler society SWF 031-032

ravel daphnis et chloe: second suite

lp issues: melodiya M10 45949 008/french furtwängler society SWF 8801-8803

cd issues: deutsche grammophon 427 7832/427 7732/471 2942/melodiya MEL 10 00712/russian compact disc RCD 25003/dante LYS 124/german furtwängler society TMK 017204/chibas restorations 1125

beethoven symphony no 6 in f op 68 "pastoral"

lp issues: melodiya D 02777-02778/M10 02777 004/rococo 2077/nippon columbia DXM 155/OZ 7586/french furtwängler society SWF 7104R/ discocorp RR 412

cd issues: french furtwängler society SWF 901/melodiya MEL 10 00712/ russian compact disc RCD 25003/membran 20.3090/20.3095/223 508/ dante LYS 064/music and arts WFSA 2001/CD 824/CD 942/tahra FURT 1004-1007/FURT 1036-1037/opus kura OPK 7001/ chibas restorations 1104

As the Staatsoper acoustic was much drier than that of the Old Philharmonie, the sound of this particular concert evening benefits from its treatment by Chibas Restorations

075 (100)/3 june 1944/reichsrundfunk recordings in vienna musikvereinssaal/*sound engineer friedrich schnapp*

wiener philharmoniker

beethoven leonore no 3 overture op 72a
lp issues: french furtwängler society SWF 7101/nippon columbia OZ 7512/japan JP 1190-1192/discocorp RR 460
cd issues: deutsche grammophon 435 3242/435 3212/474 0302/ rodolphe RPC 32522-32525/french furtwängler society SWF 901/ dante LYS 063/membran 20.3090/20.3095/223 508/preiser 90251/ music and arts CD 942/german furtwängler society TMK 200406151/ chibas restorations 1107/orfeo C834 118Y
a number of early editions were incorrectly dated 2 may 1944

mozart symphony no 40 in g minor K550
cd issues: music and arts CD 258/as-disc AS 112/membran 20.3090/ 20.3091/223 508/tahra FURT 1014-1015/german furtwängler society TMK 200406152/orfeo C834 118Y

schubert rosamunde D797: entr'acte no 3
cd issues: tahra FURT 1014-1015/german furtwängler society TMK 200406151/orfeo C834 118Y

076 (102)/7 october 1944/reichsrundfunk recordings in berlin haus des rundfunks/*sound engineer friedrich schnapp*

philharmonisches orchester berlin

mozart symphony no 39 in e flat K543

lp issues: deutsche grammophon LPM 18 725/LPM 18 8556/KL 27-32/ 2535 828/2721 202/2730 005/2740 260/heliodor 88 007/eterna 720 158

cd issues: dante LYS 246/deutsche grammophon 431 8732/439 8322/ 477 0062/membran 20.3090/20.3091/223 508/music and arts CD 954/ opus kura OPK 7018/french furtwängler society SWF 991

all editions except SWF 991 were incorrectly dated 1942-1943

bruckner symphony no 9 in d minor

lp issues: deutsche grammophon KL 27-32/LPM 18 854/2730 005/ 2740 201/heliodor 88 019/eterna 820 380

cd issues: music and arts CD 730/dante LYS 110/grammofono AB 78696-78697/deutsche grammophon 445 4182/chibas restorations 1116/pristine audio PASC 251

Pristine Audio is a clear recommendation for this important Bruckner performance

077/17 october 1944/telefunken session in vienna musikvereinssaal

wiener philharmoniker

schubert symphony no 8 "unfinished"; beethoven leonore no 2 overture

these recordings are noted in the archives of wiener philharmoniker, but they seem unlikely to have taken place

078 (103)/17 october 1944/reichsrundfunk recording in vienna musikvereinssaal/*sound engineer friedrich schnapp*

wiener philharmoniker

bruckner symphony no 8 in c minor

lp issues: unicorn UNI 109-110/deutsche grammophon 2740 201/ nippon columbia DXM 110-111

cd issues: dante LYS 106-107/grammofono AB 78696-78697/music and arts CD 764/deutsche grammophon 445 4152/chibas restorations 1115/ orfeo C834 118Y/german furtwängler society TMK 200406151

079/12 december 1944/concert recording in berlin admiralspalast/ *sound engineer friedrich schnapp*

philharmonisches orchester berlin

schubert symphony no 8 "unfinished": first movement

cd issue: tahra FURT 1008-1011/chibas restorations 1118/french furtwängler society SWF 031-032

080 (104)/19-20 december 1944/reichsrundfunk recording in vienna musikvereinssaal/*sound engineer friedrich scnapp*

wiener philharmoniker

beethoven symphony no 3 in e flat op 55 "eroica"

lp issues: urania C 7075/melodiya D 06443-06444/M10 06443 009/ unicorn UNI 104/vox turnabout THS 65020/intercord INT 120 921/ emi 3C153 53810-53816M/2C051 63332

cd issues: priceless D 16395/melodiya MEL 10 00710/russian compact disc RCD 25001/ music and arts CD 814/CD 942/documents LV 919-920/historical performers HP 2/urania (japan) URCD 7095/grammofono AB 78538/dante LYS 063/preiser 90251/ tahra FURT 1031/FURT 1034-1035/FURT 1060-1062/opus kura OPK 7026/chibas restorations 1107/orfeo C834 118Y/grand slam GS 2005

several early editions of this performance incorrectly named orchestra as berlin philharmonic

081 (105)/23 january 1945/concert recording in berlin admiralspalast/*sound engineer friedrich schnapp*

philharmonisches orchester berlin

brahms symphony no 1: fourth movement

lp issues: french furtwängler society SWF 8801-8803/japan AT 13-14

cd issues: refrain DR 91 0004/french furtwängler society SWF 951-952/ music and arts CD 805/CD 941/dante LYS 048/LYS 204/tahra FURT 1004-1007/ japanese furtwängler centre WFHC 024/chibas restorations 1109

this movement is presumably all that remains of a concert that was interrupted by a power failure following an air-raid

082 (106-107)/28 january 1945/reichsrundfunk recordings in vienna musikvereinssaal/*sound engineer friedrich schnapp*

wiener philharmoniker

franck symphony in d minor

lp issues: vox PL 7230/melodiya D 021093-021094/discocorp RR 403/ japan JP 1128-1129/french furtwängler society SWF 7302

cd issues: french furtwängler society SWF 902/dante LYS 124/arlecchino ARL 140/chibas restorations 1111/orfeo C834 118Y

brahms symphony no 2 in d op 73

lp issues: french furtwängler society SWF 7301/discocorp SID 713/RR 418/ olympic OL 8141/japan JP 1128-1129/nippon columbia OW 7821/ emi 3C153 53661-53669M

cd issues: nuova era 013 6322-6324/french furtwängler society SWF 902/ dante LYS 047/deutsche grammophon 435 3242/435 3212/music and arts CD 804/CD 941/chibas restorations 1111/orfeo C834 118Y

083 (108-109)/25 may 1947/rias concert recordings in berlin titania palast

philharmonisches orchester berlin

beethoven symphony no 6 in f op 68 "pastoral"; symphony no 5 in c minor op 67
lp issue: cetra FE 32
cd issues: cetra CDE 1014/rodolphe RPC 32422-32424/german furtwängler society TMK 08080/music and arts CD 789/CD 942 (no 5)/bellaphon 689 22003 (no 6)/tahra FURT 1016/FURT 2002-2004/dante LYS 198 (no 5)/ chibas restorations 1126/audite 21 403

This first post-war Berlin concert from Furtwängler is best heard in its latest incarnation from Audite

084 (110-111)/27 may 1947/sender freies berlin recordings in berlin haus des rundfunks

philharmonisches orchester berlin

beethoven egmont overture op 84
lp issues: deutsche grammophon LPM 18 724/LPM 18 859/004 279/2535 810/ 2721 202/2730 005/2740 260/heliodor 88 008
cd issues: deutsche grammophon 439 8322/477 0062/nuova era 013 6313/ 013 6300/french furtwängler society SWF 011-013/chibas restorations 1105

beethoven symphony no 5 in c minor op 67
lp issues: deutsche grammophon LPM 18 724/2535 810/2721 202/2730 005/ 2740 260/heliodor 88 008/heliodor (usa) H 25078/HS 25078/eterna 820 280
cd issues: deutsche grammophon 439 8322/474 7282/bellaphon 689 22003/ /french furtwängler society SWF 011-013/chibas restorations 1105

French Furtwängler Society is the best option for these vivid readings

085 (112-113)/9 june 1947/concert recordings in hamburg musikhalle/*sound engineer friedrich schnapp*

philharmonisches staatsorchester

beethoven leonore no 2 overture op 72

lp issues: discocorp RR 511/cetra FE 48/french furtwängler society SWF 8602

cd issues: nuova era 013 6303/013 6300/french furtwängler society SWF 921-922/ elaborations ELA 906/music and arts CD 869/tahra FURT 1090-1093

strauss tod und verklärung

lp issues: discocorp RR 511/cetra FE 41/french furtwängler society SWF 8602

cd issues: nuova era 013 6317/virtuoso 269 7302/originals SH 834/french furtwängler society SWF 921-922/arlecchino ARL 111-112/evangel FRL 1003/ music and arts CD 829

086 (114)/13 august 1947/concert recording in salzburg festspielhaus

wiener philharmoniker

brahms symphony no 1 in c minor op 68

cd issue: japanese furtwängler centre WFHC 024

surprisingly this has not been included in orfeo's recent complete set of furtwängler's salzburg festival concerts, therefore it has not been possible to verify if this japanese issue is genuine or if it is the lucerne performance from the same month (session 088)

087 (115)/20 august 1947/concert recording in lucerne jesuitenkirche

schweizerisches festspielorchester/luzerner festwochenchor/ elisabeth schwarzkopf/hans hotter

brahms ein deutsches requiem

lp issue: japan W 24

cd issues: wing WCD 1-2/french furtwängler society SWF 971-972

final two bars of the work missing from source: french furtwängler society adds identical bars taken from the opening movement

088 (116-118)/27 august 1947/concert recordings in lucerne kunsthaus

schweizerisches festspielorchester/adrian aeschbacher (piano)

beethoven leonore no 3 overture op 72a
lp issue: japan AT 04
cd issues: french furtwängler society SWF 961-962/music and arts CD 1018/
tahra FURT 1028-1029

beethoven piano concerto no 1 in c op 15
lp issues: rococo 2106/french furtwängler society SWF 7401/japan JPL 1006/
discocorp RR 205/RR 438/nippon columbia OZ 7595
cd issues: french furtwängler society SWF 961-962/dante LYS 199/elaborations
ELA 006/music and arts CD 839/CD 1018/tahra FURT 1028-1029

brahms symphony no 1 in c minor op 68
lp issues: french furtwängler society SWF 7601/discocorp RR 393/
nippon columbia OZ 7597
cd issues: french furtwängler society SWF 971-972/dante LYS 209-210/
music and arts CD 804/CD 1018/tahra FURT 1028-1029

Any of the editions which give us the complete concert (Music and Arts, French Furtwängler Society and Tahra) can be recommended

089 (119)/29-30 august 1947/hmv sessions in lucerne kunsthaus

schweizerisches festspielorchester/yehudi menuhin (violin)/

producer walter legge

beethoven violin concerto in d op 61

2ZA 31	DB 6574
2ZA 32	
2ZA 33	DB 6575
2ZA 34	
2ZA 35	DB 6576
2ZA 36	
2ZA 37	DB 6577
2ZA 38	
2ZA 39	DB 6578
2ZA 40	
2ZA 41	DB 6579

lp issues: emi 1C027 01570M/3C153 53800-53805M/french furtwängler society 2C051 01570/japan JP 1114

cd issues: dante LYS 249/music and arts CD 1018/testament SBT 1109/ membran 20.3090/20.3094/223 508/naxos 8.110996

78rpm edition also published in automatic coupling with numbers DB 9198-9203

wagner lohengrin prelude

2ZA 42	unpublished
2ZA 43	

cd issue: testament SBT 1141

090/16 september 1947/rehearsal recording in berlin haus des rundfunks

philharmonisches orchester berlin

brahms symphony no 2 in d op 73

cd issue: french furtwängler society SWF 062-063

091 (120-121)/16 september 1947/sender freies berlin recordings in berlin-dahlem gemeindehaus

philharmonisches orchester berlin

hindemith symphonic metamorphoses on themes of carl maria von weber

lp issues: deutsche grammophon LPM 18 857/2535 164

cd issues: dante LYS 212/deutsche grammophon 474 0302/
french furtwängler society SWF 001-002

strauss don juan

lp issues: deutsche grammophon LPM 18 960/2535 816/2548 719/2721 202

cd issues: deutsche grammophon 439 8372/474 0302/arlecchino ARL 111-112

092 (122-123)/28 september 1947/rias concert recordings in berlin titania palast

philharmonisches orchester berlin/yehudi menuhin (violin)

mendelssohn ein sommernachtstraum overture

lp issues: cetra FE 35

cd issues: german furtwängler society TMK 08080/tahra FURT 1020/
audite 21 403

beethoven violin concerto in d op 61

lp issues: cetra FE 1

cd issues: cetra CDE 1013/german furtwängler society TMK 08080/
tahra FURT 1020/music and arts CD 708/audite 21 403

It is confirmed by RIAS that the tape of Beethoven Symphony No 7 from this concert was erased

093/3 october 1947/stage recording in berlin staatsoper im admiralspalast

staatskapelle berlin/erna schlüter/margarete klose/ludwig suthaus/jaro prohaska/gottlob frick/kurt rehm/gerhard witting/hanno eschert/paul schmidtmann

wagner tristan und isolde: acts two and three

lp issues: french furtwängler society SWF 8205-8207/cetra FE 43

cd issues: french furtwängler society SWF 981-982/cetra CDE 1046/ dante LYS 194-195/radio years RY 103-104/chibas restorations 1140-1141

094/october 1947/interview recording in berlin-dahlem gemeindehaus

furtwängler speaks to the members of the berlin philharmonic

cd issue: german furtwängler society TMK 008080

095 (124)/27 october 1947/sender freies berlin recording in berlin titania palast

philharmonisches orchester berlin

strauss metamorphosen

lp issues: deutsche grammophon LPM 18 857/2535 816/2548 719

cd issues: dante LYS 212/arlecchino ARL 111-112/music and arts CD 719/ deutsche grammophon 477 0062/french furtwängler society SWF 001-002

096(126)/10-12 and 17 november 1947/hmv sessions in vienna musikvereinssaal/*producer walter legge*

wiener philharmoniker

beethoven symphony no 3 in e flat op 55 "eroica"

2VH 7068	DB 6741
2VH 7069	
2VH 7070	DB 6742
2VH 7073	
2VH 7074	DB 6743
2VH 7075	
2VH 7076	DB 6744
2VH 7077	
2VH 7078	DB 6745
2VH 7079	
2VH 7080	DB 6746
2VH 7081	
2VH 7082	DB 6747

lp issues: discocorp RR 456/japan JP 1190-1192/emi 3C153 53800-53805M/ french furtwängler society SWF 7903

cd issues: dante LYS 197/toshiba SGR 8221/tahra FURT 1027/FURT 1060-1062/ naxos 8.110995

78rpm edition was also published in automatic coupling with the numbers DB 9296-9302; side five (2VH 7074) was re-recorded on 15 february 1949

097 (125)/11, 19 and 26 november and 3 december 1947/
hmv sessions in vienna brahmssaal of the musikverein/
producer walter legge

wind soloists of the wiener philharmoniker

mozart wind serenade in b flat K361

2VH 7062	DB 6707
2VH 7063	
2VH 7064	DB 6708
2VH 7104	
2VH 7051	DB 6709
2VH 7090	
2VH 7071	DB 6710
2VH 7193	
2VH 7072	DB 6711
2VH 7089	

lp issues: electrola E 91175/WALP 579/emi 1C047 01244M/ unicorn WFS 10

cd issues: emi 763 8182/dante LYS 250/french furtwängler society SWF 991/naxos 8.110994/music and arts CD 1097/ membran 222 128

78rpm edition was also published in automatic coupling with the numbers DB 9226-9230

098 (127)/17-20 november 1947/hmv sessions in vienna musikvereinssaal/*producer walter legge*

wiener philharmoniker

brahms symphony no 1 in c minor op 68

2VH 7083 DB 6634
2VH 7084
2VH 7085 DB 6635
2VH 7086
2VH 7087 DB 6636
2VH 7088
2VH 7091 DB 6637
2VH 7092
2VH 7093 DB 6638
2VH 7099
2VH 7100 DB 6639

lp issues: hmv COLH 97/electrola E 90992/WALP 545/unicorn WFS 6/ emi 1C027 01145M/1C147 50336-50339M/1C149 53420-53426/ 2C153 53420-53426/3C153 53661-53669M

cd issues: dante LYS 205/testament SBT 1142/naxos 8.110998/ japanese furtwängler society WFFC 1401

78rpm edition was also published in automatic coupling with numbers DB 9220-9224

Clear recommendation is the CD edition from Testament

099 (128)/25 november 1947/hmv session in vienna musikvereinssaal/*producer walter legge*

wiener philharmoniker

beethoven coriolan overture op 62

2VH 7101 DB 6625/victor 11-6036
2VH 7102

lp issues: hmv FBLP 25113/unicorn WFS 9/emi 1C047 00843M/ 1C149 53432-53439M/ 2C153 52540-52551

cd issues: dante LYS 249/emi 565 5132/907 8782/naxos 8.11099

100/19-21 february 1948/rehearsal recording in berlin titania palast

philharmonisches orchester berlin

furtwängler symphony no 2: second movement

cd issue: refrain DR 92 0031

Although Furtwängler's brief verbal comments are barely audible, this is an important document by virtue of the fact that it preceded the work's premiere performance on 22 February 1948

101 (129)/22-23 and 25 march 1948/decca sessions in london kingsway hall/*producer victor olof*

london philharmonic orchestra

brahms symphony no 2 in d op 73

AR 12079 K 1875/london (usa) LA 189
AR 12080
AR 12081 K 1876/london (usa) LA 189
AR 12082
AR 12083 K 1877/london (usa) LA 189
AR 12084
AR 12085 K 1878/london (usa) LA 189
AR 12086
AR 12087 K 1879/london (usa) LA 189
AR 12088

lp issues: decca LXT 2586/ACL 50/592.109/london (usa) LLP 28/B 19020

cd issues: dante LYS 204/dutton CDEA 5204/naxos 8.111000/decca 476 2733/ japanese furtwängler centre WFFC 1402

78rpm edition was also published in automatic coupling with the numbers AK 1875-1879; a japanese cd issue on the wing label purports to contain an additional unpublished take of the side containing the opening of the second movement

As there were disagreements between conductor and recording engineers about the placing of microphones at these sessions, several commentators have dismissed the recording: however, in Dutton's CD transfer it emerges as a strong performance with familiar Furtwängler characteristics

102 (130)/25 march 1948/hmv session in london abbey road studios

philharmonia orchestra/kirsten flagstad/*producer walter legge*

wagner götterdämmerung: starke scheite schichtet mir dort

2EA 12850 DB 6792

2EA 12851

2EA 12852 DB 6793

2EA 12853

2EA 12854 DB 6794

45rpm issue: victor WHMV 1024

lp issues: hmv FALP 119/FALP 194/victor LHMV 1024/french furtwängler society SWF 7803/emi 1C147 01491-01492M/2C051 03855/EX 29 12273

cd issues: emi 565 2122/763 0302/naxos 8.110997

103 (131)/3 august 1948/stage recording in salzburg festspielhaus

wiener philharmoniker/chor der wiener staatsoper/erna schlüter/ lisa della casa/julius patzak/rudolf schock/ferdinand frantz/herbert alsen/otto edelmann/hermann gallos/karl dönch

beethoven fidelio

lp issue: rococo 1012

cd issues: melodram CDM 25009/french furtwängler society SWF 992-993

numbers 5-8 (act one) unfortunately missing from source

104/3 october 1948/concert recording in london royal albert hall

wiener philharmoniker

beethoven symphony no 2 in d op 36

lp issues: emi 2C051 03649/1C149 53432-53439M

cd issues: music and arts CD 942/emi 763 1922/763 6062/907 8782/ french furtwängler society SWF 091/pristine audio PASC 355

A controversial item in the Furtwängler discography, with many doubting its authenticity: Pristine Audio makes a more convincing argument than the earlier editions

105/18 october 1948/concert recording in hamburg musikhalle/

sound engineer friedrich schnapp

philharmonisches staatsorchester hamburg

furtwängler symphony no 2 in e minor

cd issue: french furtwängler society SWF 921-922

106 (133-134)/22 october 1948/sender freies berlin recordings in berlin-dahlem gemeindehaus

philharmonisches orchester berlin

bach orchestral suite no 3 in d BWV 1068

lp issues: deutsche grammophon LPM 18 856/KL 27-31/2535 806

cd issue: deutsche grammophon 477 0062

brahms symphony no 4 in e minor op 98

cd issues: tahra FURT 1025/japanese furtwängler centre WFHC 003

107 (135-137)/24 october 1948/rias concert recordings in berlin titania palast

philharmonisches orchester berlin

bach orchestral suite no 3 in d BWV 1068
lp issue: german furtwängler society F668.164-165
cd issues: german furtwängler society TMK 12681/music and arts CD 708/
tahra FURT 1026/audite 21.403

schubert symphony no 8 in b minor D759 "unfinished"
lp issue: vox turnabout TV 34478
cd issues: priceless D 13272/german furtwängler society TMK 12681/
audite 21.403

brahms symphony no 4 in e minor op 98
lp issues: hmv FALP 544/LXLP 121/electrola E 90995/WALP 548/unicorn WFS 1/
emi 1C047 01147M/1C147 50336-50339M/1C149 53420-53426/
2C153 53420-53426/ 3C153 53661-53669M
cd issues: as-disc AS 331-332/virtuoso 269 9072/refrain DR 91 0004/
emi 252 3212/565 5132/907 8782/chibas restorations 1145audite 21.403
refrain issue incorrectly dated 22 october 1948; emi 907 8782 incorrectly describes orchestra as wiener philharmoniker

Audite offers this entire concert programme in finely restored sound

108 (138)/2 november 1948/bbc studio recording in london

wilhelm furtwängler talks in english about conducting beethoven in an interview with h.k. brailsford
lp issues: mrf records MRF 14/japan AT 07-08
cd issues: king records (japan) KICC 2354/tahra FURT 1090-1093/
music and arts CD 792
not all editions contain the entire interview

109/3 november 1948/newsreel film recording of rehearsal in london empress hall

philharmonisches orchester berlin

brahms symphony no 4: fourth movement (incomplete)

cd issue: japanese furtwängler society WFJ 19

vhs video: teldec 4509 950383

laserdisc: teldec 4509 950386

the extract also appears in various television documentaries about furtwängler

110 (139)/12 november 1948/rehearsal recording in stockholm konserthuset

stockholms konsertförenings orkester

beethoven leonore no 3 overture op 72a

lp: french furtwängler society SWF 7101/unicorn WFS 5/emi 1C053 93533M/ 3C053 93533M/3C153 53810-53816M

cd issues: rodolphe RPC 32522-32524/bis BISCD 424A/emi 565 9152/ music and arts CD 793

111 (140-142)/13 november 1948/concert recording in stockholm konserthuset

stockholms konsertförenings orkester

beethoven symphony no 8 in f op 93

lp issues: unicorn WFS 5/olympic OL 8120/OL 8129/emi 1C149 53432-53439M/ 1C053 93533M/3C053 93533/2C153 52540-52551/ariston ARCL 13035

cd issues: music and arts CD 793/dante LYS 199/emi 763 6062/763 0342/ 907 8782/french furtw:angler society SWF 091

beethoven leonore no 3 overture op 72a

lp issues: unicorn WFS 5/emi 1C053 93533M/3C053 93533M/ 3C153 53810-53816M

cd issue: dante LYS 107

beethoven symphony no 7 in a op 92

lp issues: discocorp RR 505/nippon columbia OZ 7587

cd issues: dante LYS 198/music and arts CD 793

112 (143)/19 november 1948/concert recording in stockholm konserthuset

stockholms konsertförenings orkester/musikaliska sällskapets kör/ kerstin lindberg-torlind/bernhard sönnerstedt

brahms ein deutsches requiem

lp issues: unicorn WFS 17-18/orfeus (sweden) 1-73-4/5/ emi 1C187 93534-93535M/3C153 93534-93535M

cd issues: dante LYS 209-210/emi 252 3212/music and arts CD 289/ japanese furtwängler centre WFHC 016-017/pristine audio PACO 086

113 (144-145 and 149)/7-8 december 1948 and 15-17 february 1949/ hmv sessions in vienna musikvereinssaal/*producer walter legge*

wiener philharmoniker

mendelssohn hebrides overture

2VH 7108 DB 6941/victor 66-6024
2VH 7109
45rpm issues: hmv 7R 102/7RF 102/7RQ 102
lp issues: hmv ALP 1526/XLP 30097/FALP 617/QALP 10298/electrola E 60655/ WDLP 662/emi 1C149 03584-03586M/french furtwängler society SWF 8001
cd issues: emi 566 7702/naxos 8.110999/japanese furtwängler centre WFFC 1402

mozart symphony no 40 in g minor K550

2VH 7110 DB 6997
2VH 7111
2VH 7112 DB 6998
2VH 7113
2VH 7114 DB 6998
2VH 7115
45rpm issue: victor WHMV 1010
lp issues: hmv ALP 1498/XLP 30104/FALP 117/FALP 50033/QALP 117/ victor LHMV 1010/electrola E 90152/WALP 1498/E 91075/WALP 562/ E 70361/STE 91075/SME 91075/emi 1C027 00906M
cd issues: dante LYS 246/emi 566 7702/763 1932/907 8782/ naxos 8.110996/music and arts CD 1097

114 (147)/8 february 1949/concert recording in vienna musikvereinssaal

wiener philharmoniker/paul badura-skoda (piano)/ dagmar bella (piano)

mozart concerto for two pianos in e flat K365

cd issues: orfeo C834 118Y/music and arts CD 1097

previous issues by discocorp, french furtwängler society and music and arts are now considered not to be genuine, and paul badura-skoda himself continues to doubt the authenticity of these latest incarnations

115 (150-153 and 189)/16-17 and 22-23 february 1949 and
***31 january 1950/hmv sessions in vienna musikvereinssaal/**
producer walter legge
wiener philharmoniker

wagner siegfried idyll
2VH 7121 DB 6916
2VH 7122
2VH 7123 DB 6917
2VH 7124
lp issues: hmv FALP 110/FALP 546/QALP 10216/victor LHMV 1049/
unicorn WFS 2-3/angel seraphim 6024/emi 1C149 01197-01199M/
29 12343
cd issues: emi 252 3282/testament SBT 1141/naxos 8.110999

wagner tannhäuser overture
2VH 7125 unpublished
2VH 7126
2VH 7127 unpublished
cd issue: testament SBT 1141

*wagner götterdämmerung: trauermusik
2VH 7133 DB 6946
2VH 7134
45rpm issues: hmv 7R 151/7RF 149/7RQ 3011/7RW 124/victor EHB 2
lp issues: hmv FALP 194/victor LHMV 1049/emi 2C051 03855/
french furtwängler society SWF 7803
cd issue: testament SBT 1141

wagner götterdämmerung: siegfrieds rheinfahrt
2VH 7135 DB 6949
2VH 7136
2VH 7137 DB 6950
lp issues: hmv FALP 110/FALP 194/COLH 307/electrola SME 91399/
victor LHMV 1049/french furtwängler society SWF 7803/emi 2C051 03855
cd issue: testament SBT 1141

116 (154)/14 march 1949/sender freies berlin recording in berlin-dahlem gemeindehaus

philharmonisches orchester berlin

bruckner symphony no 8 in c minor

cd issue: testament SBT 1143

previous issues of this performance (hmv FALP 850-851/electrola STE 91375-91378/SMVP 8057-8058/emi 1C147 29231-29232/dante LYS 244) are now considered to be a conflation of the two peformances on 14 and 15 march

117 (155)/15 march 1949/rias concert recording in berlin titania palast

philharmonisches orchester berlin

bruckner symphony no 8 in c minor

lp issues: rococo 2032/discocorp RR 457/nippon columbia OS 7091-7092

cd issues: arkadia CDWFE 356/palladio PD 4135/german furtwängler society MMS 9103/originals SH 854/dante LYS 245/evangel FRL 1001/music and arts CD 624/emi 566 2102/audite 21 403

see also the note for session 116 above

118 (156-159)/30-31 march and 2 april 1949/hmv sessions in vienna musikvereinssaal/*producer walter legge*

wiener philharmoniker

wagner der fliegende holländer overture

2VH 7128 DB 6975/ED 1233

2VH 7129

2VH 7130 DB 6976/ED 1234

lp issues: hmv FALP 289/FALP 30039/electrola E 90023/WALP 534/E 91074/ WALP 561/ columbia (austria) VALP 538/unicorn WFS 2-3/angel seraphim 6024/ melodiya D 0132137-0132138/emi 29 12343/1C149 01197-01199M

cd issues: historical perforners HP 4/emi 252 3282/764 9352/ naxos 8.110997/praga digitals sacd 350107

78rpm edition was also published in automatic coupling with numbers DB 9727-9728

wagner die walküre: walkürenritt

2VH 7131 DB 6950

45rpm issues: 7R 141/7P 206/7RF 203/7RQ 3004/7RW 125/victor EHA 17

lp issues: hmv FBLP 25057/victor LHMV 1049/unicorn WFS 2-3/ angel seraphim 6024/emi 29 12343/1C149 01197-01199M

cd issues: emi 252 3282/764 9352/naxos 8.110997/membran 222 128/ tahra FURT 1026/archipel ARPCD 0261

emi 252 3282 was incorrectly dated 1954

berlioz la damnation de faust: marche hongroise

2VH 7132 unpublished

lp issue: emi 1C149 03584-03586M

cd issue: emi 566 7702

118/concluded

brahms haydn variations op 56a

2VH 7157 DB 6932
2VH 7158
2VH 7164 DB 6933
2VH 7165
2VH 7166 DB 6934

45rpm issue: victor WHMV 1010

lp issues: hmv ALP 1011/FALP 188/QALP 188/electrola E 90025/WALP 1011/ E 70420/WBLP 558/columbia (austria) VALP 505/victor LHMV 1010/ emi 3C153 53661-53669M/1C047 01415M

cd issues: flowers BL 024/dante LYS 206/emi 252 3212/565 5132/907 8782/ naxos 8.110998/japanese furtwängler centre WFFC 1401

78rpm edition was also published in automatic coupling with numbers DB 9402-9404; flowers BL 024 and emi 252 3212 were incorrectly dated january 1952

119 (160-165)/1 and 4 april 1949/hmv sessions in vienna musikvereinssaal/*producer walter legge*

wiener philharmoniker

mozart serenade no 13 in g K525 "eine kleine nachtmusik"

2VH 7159 DB 6911
2VH 7160
2VH 7161 DB 6912
2VH 7162

45rpm issues: hmv 7R 122-123/ERF 17013/electrola E 50063/7ERW 5315/ victor 11-7965-7966/WHMV 1018

lp issues: hmv ALP 1498/XLP 30104/FALP 117/FALP 30033/QALP 117/ victor LHMV 1018/ electrola E 90152/WALP 1498/E 60543/WDLP 601/E 80801/ SME 80801/WCLP 854/HZE 105/SHZE 105/emi 1C149 03584-03586M

cd issues: emi 763 8182/naxos 8.110994

119/concluded

wagner die meistersinger von nürnberg overture

2VH 7163 DB 6942

2VH 7169

2VH 7170 DB 6943

lp issues: hmv FALP 289/FALP 546/FALP 30039/FALP 30213/QALP 10216/
electrola E 90023/WALP 534/E 80801/WCLP 854/E 91074/WALP 561/
SME 80801/E 83388/WCLP 820/HZE 105/SHZE 105/columbia (austria) VALP 538/
victor LHMV 1049/unicorn WFS 2-3/angel seraphim 6024/emi 29 12343/
1C149 01197-01199M

cd issues: historical performers HP 4/emi 252 3282/764 9352/
naxos 8.110997/membran 222 128/praga digitals sacd 350 107

wagner die meistersinger von nürnberg: tanz der lehrbuben

2VH 7171 DB 6943

45rpm issues: hmv 7R 141/7P 206/7RF 203/7RQ 3004/7RW 125/victor EHA 17

lp issues: victor LHMV 1049/unicorn WFS 2-3/emi 29 12343/
1C149 01197-01199M

cd issues: emi 252 3282/764 9352/naxos 8.110997/praga digitals sacd 350 107

brahms hungarian dances nos 1 in g minor, 3 in f and 10 in e

2VH 7167 DB 6934/DB 9402

2VH 7168 DB 6976/DB 9727/ED 1233

45rpm issue: victor EHA 17 (nos 1 and 10)

lp issues: unicorn WFS 1/emi 1C149 03584-03586M/1C149 53420-53426/
2C153 53420-53426/3C153 53661-53669M

cd issues: dante LYS 204/emi 252 3212/565 5132/naxos 8.110999/
membran 222 128/pristine audio PASC 240

120 (167-169)/10 june 1949/concert recording in wiesbaden kurhaus

philharmonisches orchester berlin

pfitzner three palestrina preludes

lp issues: rococo 2034/german furtwängler society F666.156-157/
discocorp RR 457/cetra FE 26/nippon columbia OZ 7598-7599

cd issues: as-disc AS 370/tahra FURT 1021-1022

mozart symphony no 40 in g minor K550

lp issues: german furtwängler society F666.156-157/discocorp RR 395/
cetra FE 18/nippon columbia OZ 7598-7599

cd issues: cetra CDE 1015/CDE 3009/virtuoso 269.7352/
tahra FURT 1021-1022

brahms symphony no 4 in e minor op 98

lp issues: german furtwängler society F666.156-157/discocorp RR 394

cd issues: nippon columbia OZ 7598-7599/dante LYS 206/
elaborations ELA 903/tahra FURT 1021-1022

Tahra is the clear recommendation here, giving us the entire concert

121 (170)/27 july 1949/stage recording in salzburg felsenreitschule

wiener philharmoniker/chor der wiener staatsoper/irmgard seefried/
wilma lipp/walther ludwig/karl schmitt-walter/peter klein/josef greindl/
paul schöffler/gertrud grob-prandl/sieglinde wagner/elisabeth höngen/
elisabeth rutgers/ruthilde boesch/polly batic/edith oravez/ernst
haefliger/hermann uhde/hermann gallos/karl dönch

mozart die zauberflöte

lp issues: unique opera recordings EJS 572/nippon columbia OZ 7572-7574/
discocorp IGI 337

cd issues: arlecchino ARL 78-80/music and arts CD 882/orfeo C650 053D

Orfeo presents us with an official Salzburg Festival edition of this remarkable performance

122 (172)/3 august 1949/concert recording in salzburg festspielhaus

wiener philharmoniker

pfitzner symphony in c op 46

lp issues: rococo 2109/discocorp RR 437/cetra FE 26/nippon columbia OZ 7593

cd issues: as-disc AS 370/dante LYS 212/german furtwängler society TMK 10670/ theatre 400 3531/orfeo C409 048L

123/18 august 1949/interview recording in salzburg mozarteum

furtwängler speaks on the subject of creative and non-creative artists (composer and conductor)

cd issues: german furtwängler society TMK 10670/orfeo SF 012

124 (173)/24 august 1949/concert recordings in lucerne kunsthaus

schweizerisches festspielorchester/wolfgang schneiderhan (violin)/ enrico mainardi (cello)

brahms double concerto in a minor op 102

lp issue: japan W 19

cd issues: as-disc AS 372/music and arts CD 1018/japanese furtwängler centre WFHC 003

tchaikovsky symphony no 4 in f minor op 36

cd issue: french furtwängler society WFGFJ 124

The Tchaikovsky is the most recent addition to the Furtwängler discography, anticipating by eighteen months the conductor's commercial recording of the work

125 (174)/29-31 august 1949/hmv sessions in lucerne kunsthaus

schweizerisches festspielorchester/yehudi menuhin (violin)/

producer walter legge

wagner lohengrin prelude

2ZA 61 unpublished

2ZA 62

brahms violin concerto in d op 77

2ZA 63 DB 21000/victor DM 1361

2ZA 64

2ZA 65 DB 21001/victor DM 1361

2ZA 66

2ZA 67 DB 21002/victor DM 1361

2ZA 68

2ZA 69 DB 21002/victor DM 1361

2ZA 70

2ZA 71 DB 21003/victor DM 1361

45rpm issue: victor WDM 1361

lp issues: hmv FALP 122/FALP 30001/electrola E 90013/WALP 524/victor LM 1142/emi HLM 7015/1C047 01239M/1C149 53420-53426/ 2C153 53420-53426/2C051 01239M/3C153 53661-53669M

cd issues: movimento musica 051.052/emi 252 3212/763 4962/907 8782/ naxos 8.110999/pristine audio PASC 342

early editions of this recording were incorrectly dated 7 october 1949

126 (175-177)/18 october 1949/sender freies berlin recordings in berlin-dahlem gemeindehaus

philharmonisches orchester berlin/ludwig hoelscher (cello)

beethoven leonore no 2 overture op 72
lp issues: deutsche grammophon LPM 18 742/LPM 18 859/2535 807/2730 005/
heliodor 88 008/melodiya D 26585-26586
cd issues: deutsche grammophon 477 0062/french furtwängler society
SWF 011-013/chibas restorations 1130

karl hoeller cello concerto no 2
lp issue: cetra FE 31
cd issue: originals SH 834/french furtwängler society SWF 001=002

bruckner symphony no 7 in e
lp issues: hmv FALP 852-853/electrola STE 91375-91378/SMVP 8055-8056/
emi HQM 1169/F666.700/1C147 29229-29230
cd issues: dante LYS 214/emi 566 2062/french furtwängler society SWF 051/
pristine audio/chibas restorations 1129

127 (178-182)/18-19 december 1949/rias concert recordings in berlin titania palast

philharmonisches orchester berlin/gerhard taschner (violin)

schumann manfred overture op 115
lp issue: deutsche grammophon 2535 805
cd issues: deutsche grammophon 415 6612/427 4042/474 0302/
virtuoso 269,7402/arlecchino ARL 151-152/audite 21 403

brahms symphony no 3 in f op 90
lp issues: hmv FALP 543/electrola E 90994/WALP 547/unicorn WFS 4/
emi 1C027 01146M/1C147 50336-50339M/1C149 53420-53426/
2C153 53420-53426/3C153 53661-53669M
cd issues: virtuoso 269 9072/emi 252 3212/565 5132/907 8782/
audite 21 403
emi 907 8782 incorrectly describes orchestra as wiener philharmoniker and recording date as 8 december 1949

wolfgang fortner violin concerto
lp issue: cetra FE 31
cd issues: as-disc AS 370/german furtwängler society TMK 12681/
audite 21 403

wagner götterdämmerung: trauermusik; meistersinger overture
lp issues: deutsche grammophon 2535 806/2721 113/2721 202/
2740 260
cd issues: deutsche grammophon 415 6632/427 4062/439 8372/
474 0302/479 1148/archipel ARPCD 0261 (meistersinger)/
audite 21 403

Audite conveniently presents us with this entire concert programme

128 (184-186 and 188)/18-24 january 1950/hmv sessions in vienna musikvereinssaal/*producer walter legge*

wiener philharmoniker

beethoven symphony no 7 in a op 92

2VH 7180 DB 21106
2VH 7181
2VH 7182 DB 21107
2VH 7183
2VH 7184 DB 21108
2VH 7185
2VH 7186 DB 21109
2VH 7187
2VH 7188 DB 21110
2VH 7189

45rpm issue: victor WHMV 1008

lp issues: hmv ALP 115/FALP 30031/UVT 3031/QALP 115/victor LHMV 1008/ electrola E 90016/WALP 527/SME 90016/SMVP 8048/angel seraphim 6018/ emi 1C 027 00809M/1C149 53432-53439M/2C153 52540-52551/2C051 03089

cd issues: emi 763 6062/769 8032/907 8782

78rpm edition was also published in automatic coupling with numbers DB 9516-9520

schubert symphony no 8 in b minor D759 "unfinished"

2VH 7190 DB 21131
2VH 7191
2VH 7192 DB 21132
2VH 7193
2VH 7194 DB 21133
2VH 7195

45rpm issue: victor WHMV 1020

lp issues: hmv FALP 317/FALP 30043/FBLP 1005/electrola E 90153/WALP 1500/ E 60550/WDLP 603/SME 91486/SMVP 8040/victor LHMV 1020/emi XLP 30104/ 1C047 00907M/2C051 02614

cd issues: emi 747 1202/763 1932/565 9172/565 9152/566 7702/ membran 222 128/naxos 8.111344

78rpm edition was also published in automatic coupling with numbers DB 9538-9540

128/concluded

strauss tod und verklärung

2VH 7196 DB 21169

2VH 7197

2VH 7198 DB 21170

2VH 7199

2VH 7200 DB 21172

2VH 7201

45rpm issue: victor WHMV 1023

lp issues: hmv FALP 546/QALP 10216/electrola HZEL 71/victor LHMV 1023/ angel seraphim 60094/emi HQM 1137/10 11551/1C049 01155M

cd issues: emi 565 1972/907 8782/praga digitals sacd 350100

78rpm edition was also published in automatic coupling with numbers DB 9592-9594

johann strauss kaiserwalzer

2VH 7202 DB 21174

2VH 7203

45rpm issues: hmv 7RF 104/7RQ 104

lp issues: hmv ALP 1526/XLP 30106/FALP 617/electrola SMVP 8016/ french furtwängler society SWF 8001

cd issues: deutsche grammophon 435 3352/emi 566 7702

129 (187)/25 and 30 january 1950/hmv sessions in vienna musikvereinssaal/*producer walter legge*

wiener philharmoniker

beethoven symphony no 4 in b flat op 60

2VH 7207	DB 21099
2VH 7208	
2VH 7209	DB 21100
2VH 7204	
2VH 7205	DB 21101
2VH 7206	
2VH 7210	DB 21102
2VH 7211	
2VH 7212	DB 21103
2VH 7213	

lp issues: hmv FALP 116/discocorp RR 437/french furtwängler society SWF 7904/emi 3C153 53800-53805M

cd issues: grand slam GS 2028/naxos 8.112025

78rpm edition was also published in automatic coupling with numbers DB 9524-9528; grand slam edition also includes movements 3 and 4 taken from FALP 116

130 (190-195)/1-3 february 1950/hmv sessions in vienna musikvereinssaal/*producer walter legge*

wiener philharmoniker

wagner die meistersinger von nürnberg: act three prelude

OVH 475 unpublished

OVH 476

lp issues: unicorn WFS 2-3/japan JP 1114/emi 29 12343/1C149 01197-01199M

cd issues: historical performers HP 4/emi 764 9352/naxos 8.110997

tchaikovsky serenade for strings: waltz and finale

2VH 7215 DB 21173

2VH 7218 DB 21172/ED 1227

2VH 7219

45rpm issues: hmv 7ER 5001/7R 134 (waltz)/7R 140 (finale)/7RF 148 (waltz)/ 7RF 146 (finale)/7ERF 131/7RQ 3032 (waltz)/7RQ 3002 (finale)/7ERQ 110/ electrola E 50033/7ERW 5001/7RW 101 (waltz)/7RW 123 (finale)/victor EHA 9

lp issues: hmv ALP 1526/FALP 617/electrola SMVP 8016/unicorn WFS 7/ emi 1C149 03584-03586M

cd issue: emi 764 8552

weber oberon overture

2VH 7216 DB 21104/ED 1246

2VH 7217

45rpm issues: hmv 7RF 258/7RQ 258

lp issues: hmv ALP 1526/XLP 30090/FALP 617/QALP 10298/electrola E 60655/ WDLP 662/SMVP 8016/melodiya M10 41233-41234/emi F666.699/ 1C149 03584-03586M

cd issues: palladio PD 4124/historical performers HP 8/emi 566 7702

schubert rosamunde: ballet music no 2 and entr'acte no 3

2VH 7220 DB 21192/electrola DB 11530

2VH 7221

45rpm issues: hmv 7R 121/7RF 143/7RQ 3012/electrola 7RW 122/ victor WHMV 1020

lp issues: hmv FALP 317/FALP 30043/electrola E 90153/WALP 1500/E 70420/ WBLP 558/victor LHMV 1020/emi XLP 30106/1C149 03584-03586M/ 2C051 03614

cd issues: emi 763 1932/566 7702

131 (196)/3 february 1950/hmv session in brahmssaal of the vienna musikverein/*producer walter legge*

wiener philharmoniker/wilma lipp

johann and josef strauss pizzicato polka

2VH 7222 DB 21173

45rpm issues: hmv 7R 134/7ER 5001/7ERF 131/7RF 148/7RQ 3032/
7ERQ 110/ electrola E 50033/7RW 101/7ERW 5001

lp issues: emi XLP 30106/1C149 03584-03586M

cd issue: emi 566 7702

two different takes of the 78rpm recording, one with standard triangle part and one without, seem to have been in circulation

mozart die zauberflöte: der hölle rache; o zittre nicht mein lieber sohn!

2VH 7223 unpublished

2VH 7224

lp issues: emi RLS 764/1C137 43187-43189M/japan AT 13-14/
french furtwängler society SWF 8601

cd issue: emi 566 7702

132 (197)/4 march 1950/stage recording in milan teatro alla scala

orchestra del teatro alla scala/ferdinand frantz/elisabeth höngen/walburga wegener/margarete weth-falke/angelo mattiello/günther treptow/joachim sattler/albert emmerich/alois pernerstorfer/emil markwort/magda gabory/margherita kenney/sieglinde wagner

wagner das rheingold

lp issues: unique opera recordings UORC 128/discocorp RR 420/everest S-473/
murray hill 940 477/cetra CFE 101/FE 37

cd issues: cetra CDC 26/arkadia CDWFE 301/CDWFE 351/virtuoso 269 7282/
269 9082/music and arts CD 914/gebhardt JGCD 0018/archipel ARPCD 0413/
french furtwängler society SWF 111-124/pristine audio/chibas restorations

Both Pristine Audio and Chibas Restorations achieve far better sonic results than any of the previous versions

133 (198)/9 march 1950/stage recording in milan teatro alla scala
orchestra del teatro alla scala/kirsten flagstad/hilde konetzni/ elisabeth höngen/günther treptow/ferdinand frantz/ludwig weber/ ilona steingruber/walburga wegener/karen marie crkall/dagmar schmedes/margherita kenney/margret weth-falke/polly batic/ sieglinde wagner
wagner die walküre
lp issues: ed smith EJS 534/discocorp RR 420/murray hill 940 477/everest S-474/ cetra LO 86/CFE 101/FE 38
cd issues: cetra CDC 15/arkadia CDWFE 301/CDWFE 351/virtuoso 269 9082/ 269 9102/music and arts CD 914/archipel ARPCD 0414/gebhardt JGCD 0018/ french furtwängler society SWF 111-124/pristine audio/chibas restorations

See comment for Session no. 132 above

134 (199)/22 march 1950/stage recording in milan teatro alla scala
orchestra del teatro alla scala/kirsten flagstad/elisabeth höngen/julia moor/set svanholm/emil markwort/josef hermann/ludwig weber/ alois pernerstorfer
wagner siegfried
lp issues: unique opera recordings UORC 123/discocorp RR 420/everest S-475/ murray hill 940 477/cetra FE 39/CFE 101
cd issues: cetra CDC 27/arkadia CDWFE 301/CDWFE 351/virtuoso 269 9082/ 269 9092/music and arts CD 914/archipel ARPCD 4015/gebhardt JGCD 0018/ french furtwängler society SWF 111-124/pristine audio/chibas restorations

See comment for Session no. 132 above

135 (200)/4 april 1950/stage recording in milan teatro alla scala

orchestra e coro del teatro alla scala/kirsten flagstad/hilde konetzni/ elisabeth höngen/max lorenz/josef hermann/alois pernerstorfer/ marget weth-falke/margherita kenney/magda gabory/ sieglinde wagner

wagner götterdämmerung

lp issues: ed smith EJS 538/discocorp RR 420/murray hill 940 477/everest S-476/ cetra CFE 101/FE 40

cd issues: cetra CDC 28/arkadia CDWFE 301/CDWFE 351/CDWFE 364/ virtuoso 269 9112/269 9082/music and arts CD 914/gebhardt JGCD 0018/ archpiel ARPCD 0016/french furtwängler society SWF 111-124/ pristine audio/chibas restorations

CDWFE 364 claimed to be taken from the performance on 2 april 1950, but conclusive proof of this cannot be found

See comment for Session no. 132 above

136/14 and 23 april and 5 may 1950/concert recordings in buenos aires teatro colon

orquesta del teatro colon

handel concerto grosso in d minor op 6 no 10; haydn symphony no 104 in d "london"; schubert rosamunde: ballet music no 2 and entr'acte no 3; juan jose castro obertura para una opera comica

lp issue: japan AT 03

cd issues: refrain DR 92 0032/british furtwängler society WFSUK 2004 (rosamunde)

Interesting documents from Furtwängler's first South American visit, but unfortunately preserved in acetate recordings obviously taken down from a low quality radio transmission; parts of the Haydn Symphony seem to be from a clearer tape source

137/2 may 1950/concert recording in buenos aires teatro colon

orquesta y coro del teatro colon/anton dermota/angelo mattiello/ nilda hofmann/margarete klose/josef greindl/carlos feller/victor bacciato/maria del ecignard

bach matthäus-passion BWV 244

lp issue: japan AT 15-16

cd issues: archipel ARPCD 0286/japanese furtwängler centre WFHC 005-006

soloists sing in german but choir sings in spanish

AT 15-16 and ARPCD 0286 are heavily abridged editons

138 (201)/22 may 1950/concert recordings in london royal albert hall

philharmonia orchestra/kirsten flagstad

strauss vier letzte lieder

lp issues: ed smith EJS 432/cetra LO 501/FE 41/rococo 5380/vox turnabout THS 65116/TV 34830

cd issues: melodram CDM 25009/arlecchino ARL 111-112/simax PSC 1823/ eklipse EKRCD 15/testament SBT 1410/pristine audio

wagner tristan und isolde: vorspiel und liebestod; wagner götterdämmerung: siegfrieds rheinfahrt and starke scheite schichtet mir dort

cd issue: testament SBT 1410

All previous editions of the Vier letzte Lieder were truncated and transferred from poor quality acetates: only with the appearance of the Testament CD can they (and most of the rest of the concert) be heard in acceptable sound quality. The significance of the occasion cannot be overemphasised: the world premiere of the Strauss songs, Furtwängler's first public concert with the Philharmonia Orchestra and the one hundred and thirty-seventh birthday of Richard Wagner

139 (202-203)/11 june 1950/rehearsal and interview recordings in bremen grosser glockensaal

philharmonisches orchester berlin

beethoven leonore no 2 overture op 72

lp issues: french furtwängler society SWF 8602/japan GMV 108/AT 07-08

cd issues: refrain DR 92 0031/french furtwängler society SWF 921-922

this dimly recorded extract is of only four minutes duration

furtwängler talks with an unnamed interviewer about his philosophy of music and about the planning of programmes

lp issue: french furtwängler society SWF 8602

cd issue: french furtwängler society SWF 921-922

140 (204)/18 june 1950/sender freies berlin recording in berlin titania palast

philharmonisches orchester berlin

schubert symphony no 9 in c D944 "great"

lp issue: japan AT 05-06

cd issue: refrain DR 92 0023

141 (205-208)/20 june 1950/rias concert recordings in berlin titania palast

philharmonisches orchester berlin

handel concerto grosso in d minor op 6 no 10
lp issues: deutsche grammophon 2535 806/japan P 1001
cd issues: virtuoso 269.7402/audite 21 403

brahms haydn variations op 56a
lp issues: deutsche grammophon 2535 164/cetra FE 16
cd issues: deutsche grammophon 415 6622/427 4022/474 0302/
virtuoso 269.9072/french furtwängler society SWF 062-064/audite 21 403

hindemith konzert für orchester
lp issues: cetra FE 22/nippon columbia OZ 7593
cd issues: cetra CDE 1049/virtuoso 269.7322/music and arts CD 713/
german furtwängler society MMS 9010/audite 21 403

beethoven symphony no 3 in e flat op 55 "eroica"
lp issue: victor (japan) RCL 3334
cd issues: german furtwängler society MMS 9010/tahra FURT 1030/
music and arts CD 711/audite 21 403

Another complete concert presented in excellent sound by Audite

142 (209)/22 june 1950/rias interview recording in berlin hochschule für musik

furtwängler talks to an audience of students
lp issues: deutsche grammophon KL 29-32/004 279/2720 202/
2730 005/2740 260
cd issues: deutsche grammophon 477 0062/audite 21 403

143 (210-212)/13 july 1950/vara concert recordings in amsterdam concertgebouw

concertgebouworkest

beethoven symphony no 1 in c op 21
lp issues: olympic OL 8120/OL 8124/japan JP 1199-1200/dial discos 50.200
cd issues: refrain DR 92 0033/tahra FURT 1012-1013

beethoven leonore no 3 overture op 72a
lp issues: japan JP 1199-1200/AT 09-10
cd issues: refrain DR 92 0033/music and arts WFSA 2001/CD 824/
tahra FURT 1012-1013

brahms symphony no 1 in c minor op 68
lp issue: japan JP 1199-1200
cd issues: music and arts CD 289/refrain DR 92 0033/tahra FURT 1012-1013

The complete concert experience in good sound from Tahra

144 (213)/27 july 1950/stage recording in salzburg festspielhaus

wiener philharmoniker/chor der wiener staatsoper/elisabeth schwarzkopf/ljuba welitsch/irmgard seefried/tito gobbi/anton dermota/erich kunz/alfred poell

mozart don giovanni
lp issues: ed smith EJS 419/olympic 9109/discocorp RR 407/vox turnabout
THS 65154-65156/melodram MEL 713
cd issues: victor (japan) R30C 1014-1016/priceless D 16581/laudis LCD 34001/
emi 566 5672/chibas restorations 1132-1134
lp side three in olympic 9109 derived from a later 1953 performance

Chibas Restorations presents us with a clean sound picture of a recording which in some earlier incarnations was somewhat constricted

145 (218)/5 august 1950/stage recording in salzburg festspielhaus

wiener philharmoniker/chor der wiener staatsoper/kirsten flagstad/ elisabeth schwarzkopf/julius patzak/anton dermota/josef greindl/ paul schoeffler/hans braun/hermann gallos/ljubomir pantscheff

beethoven fidelio

lp issues: morgan records MOR 5001/mrf records MRF 50/bjr records BJR 112/ discocorp IGI 328/cetra FE 44/cls records AMDRL 32819

cd issues: arkadia CDWFE 304/CDWFE 354/verona 27044-27045/emi 764 9012/ opus kura OPK 7004-7005/chibas restorations 1135-1136

146 (215-216)/15 august 1950/concert recordings in salzburg festspielhaus

wiener philharmoniker

stravinsky symphony in three movements

lp issue: cetra FE 14

cd issues: varese sarabande VCD 47259/cetra CDE 1043/virtuoso 269.7322/ german furtwängler society TMK 2196/orfeo C409 048L

brahms symphony no 4 in e minor op 98

cd issues: music and arts CD 258/nuova era 013.6332-6334/orfeo C409 048L

147/16 august 1950/stage recording in salzburg felsenreitschule

wiener philharmoniker/chor der wiener staatsoper/irmgard seefried/ wilma lipp/hedda heusser/walther ludwig/erich kunz/josef greindl/ paul schoeffler/peter klein/annelies kupper/sieglinde wagner/ elisabeth höngen/hannelore steffek/luise leitner/friedl meusburger/ fred liewehr/franz höbling

mozart die zauberflöte: extracts from act two

cd issue: japanese furtwängler centre WFHC 012

it is assumed that these extracts derive from the soundtrack of filmed newsreel

148/26 august 1950/concert recording in lucerne kunsthaus

schweizerisches festspielorchester/festwochenchor/elisabeth schwarzkopf/frans vroons/hans hotter/alois pernerstorfer

berlioz la damnation de faust

lp issue: cetra FE 21

cd issues: eklipse EKR 60/japanese furtwängler society WFJ 41-42

As recent attempts have been made to improve sound quality on various 1950s Lucerne Festival performances, it is hoped that efforts can be made to obtain better results for this performance

149 (219-221)/31 august 1950/concert recordings in salzburg festspielhaus

wiener philharmoniker/willi boskovsky (violin)/josef niedermayer (flute)/wilhelm furtwängler (piano)

bach brandenburg concerti nos 3 BWV 1048 and 5 BWV 1050

lp issues: discocorp RR 515/nippon columbia OZ 7594

cd issues: refrain DR 92 0018/emi 587 4222/orfeo C409 048L/ german furtwängler society TMK 2196

beethoven symphony no 3 in e flat op 55 "eroica"

cd issues: emi 587 4222/orfeo C409 048L

150 (222-227)/25 september 1950/concert recordings in stockholm konserthuset

wiener philharmoniker

swedish national anthem; austrian national anthem
lp issues: japan GC 570234-57035/AT 13-14
cd issues: theatre 400 3531 (swedish)/japanese furtwängler centre WFHC 009-010

haydn symphony no 94 in g "surprise"
lp issues: discocorp RR 399/japan GC 570234-570235/nippon columbia OS 7075
cd issues: music and arts CD 802/japanese furtwängler centre WFHC 009-010

sibelius en saga
lp issues: japan GC 570234-570235/discocorp RR 403/RR 507
cd issues: theatre 400 3531/music and arts CD 799/japanese furtwängler centre WFHC 009-010

strauss don juan
lp issues: japan GC 570234-570235/discocorp RR 460
cd issues: music and arts CD 802/japanese furtwängler centre WFHC 009-010

beethoven symphony no 5 in c minor op 67
lp issues: japan GC 570234-570235/JP 1190-1192/discocorp RR 507/ nippon columbia OZ 7585
cd issue: music and arts CD 802/japanese furtwängler centre WFHC 009-010

151 (229)/1 october 1950/concert recording in copenhagen odd fellow palaet

wiener philharmoniker

beethoven symphony no 5 in c minor op 67
lp issue: danacord DACO 114
cd issue: danacord DACOCD 301/tahra FURT 1090-1093
recording of schubert unfinished symphony from this concert cannot be verified

152 (230-231)/3-4, 8-10 and 17 january 1951/hmv sessions in vienna musikvereinsssaal/*producer walter legge*

wiener philharmoniker

schubert rosamunde overture D 644

2VH 7233 unpublished
2VH 7234
2VH 7235 unpublished
lp issues: hmv FALP 317/FALP 30043/electrola E 90153/WALP 1500/E 70420/ WBLP 558/emi XLP 30097/2C051 03614/1C149 03584-03586M/F666.699
cd issues: emi 763 1932/566 7702

tchaikovsky symphony no 4 in f minor op 36

2VH 7236 DB 21376/unpublished
2VH 7237
2VH 7238 DB 21377/unpublished
2VH 7239
2VH 7240 DB 21378/unpublished
2VH 7241
2VH 7242 DB 21379/unpublished
2VH 7243
2VH 7244 DB 21380/unpublished
2VH 7245
2VH 7246 DB 21381/unpublished
45rpm issue: victor WHMV 1005
lp issues: hmv ALP 1025/ENC 109/FALP 120/electrola E 90030/WALP 1025/ columbia (austria) VALP 515/victor LHMV 1005/LCT 1018/unicorn WFS 7/ melodiya D 078793-078794
cd issues: palladio PD 4124/historical performers HP 8/emi 764 8552/ membran 222 128/tahra FURT 1099-1100

As the recordings in these sessions were now being made on tape, the allocated 78rpm matrix and catalogue numbers were no longer needed

153 (232)/7 january 1951/concert recording in vienna musikvereinssaal

wiener philharmoniker/wiener singakademie/irmgard seefried/rosette anday/julius patzak/otto edelmann

beethoven symphony no 9 in d minor op 125

lp issue: cetra FE 33

cd issues: cetra CDC 1/bellaphon 689 22005/orfeo C834 118Y

154 (233-234)/11-12 and 17 january 1951/hmv sessions in vienna musikvereinssaal/*producer walter legge*

wiener philharmoniker

cherubini anacreon overture

2VH 7247 DB 21493/hmv (argentina) 266 601

2VH 7248

lp issues: hmv ALP 1498/electrola E 90152/WALP 1498/E 70361/ WBLP 547/emi 1C149 03584-03586M

cd issues: emi 566 7702/907 8782

haydn symphony no 94 in g "surprise"

2VH 7249 DB 21506

2VH 7250

2VH 7252

2VH 7253 DB 21508

2VH 7254

45rpm issue: victor WHMV 1018

lp issues: hmv ALP 1011/FALP 188/FBLP 25034/QALP 188/electrola E 90025/WALP 1011/E 91075/WALP 562/STE 91075/SME 91075/ SMVP 8053/columbia (austria) VALP 505/victor LHMV 1018/ emi 1C027 00906M/unicorn WFS 11

cd issues: emi 566 7702/907 8782/grand slam GS 2028

155 (235)/18 january 1951/hmv session in vienna musikvereinssaal

wiener philharmoniker/*producer walter legge*

nicolai die lustigen weiber von windsor overture

2VH 7255 DB 21502

2VH 7256

45rpm issues: victor WHMV 1020/EHA 9

lp issues: hmv ALP 1526/XLP 30097/FALP 617/QALP 10298/electrola E 60655/ WALP 662/SMVP 8016/victor LHMV 1020/emi 1C149 03584-03586M

cd issues: 764 2942/764 2982/566 7702

156 (236-237)/24-25 january 1951/hmv sessions in vienna musikvereinssaal/*producer walter legge*

wiener philharmoniker

smetana ma vlast: the moldau

2VH 7257 DB 9787

2VH 7258 DB 9788

2VH 7262 DB 9789

45rpm issues: hmv 7ERF 153/ERF 17023/electrola E 41130/7EGW 8596/ victor WHMV 1023

lp issues: hmv BLP 1009/XLP 30106/FBLP 1046/FBLP 25024/QBLP 5006/ QALP 10298/electrola E 70023/WBLP 1009/E 60543/WDLP 601/E 80801/ WCLP 854/SME 80801/HZE 105/SHZE 105/columbia (austria) VBLP 802/ victor LHMV 1023/emi 1C149 03584-03586M/2C053 01193/F666.702

cd issues: palladio PD 4122/historical performers HP 14/emi 764 2942/ 764 2982/565 1972/membran 222 128

156/concluded

schumann manfred overture op 115

2VH 7263 DB 9789

2VH 7264 DB 9788

2VH 7265 DB 9786

45rpm issue: victor WHMV 1023

lp issues: hmv BLP 1009/XLP 30097/FBLP 1046/QBLP 5006/electrola E 70023/ WBLP 1009/E 70362/WBLP 546/E 60661/WDLP 667/columbia (austria) VBLP 802/victor LHMV 1023/emi 1C047 01415M

cd issues: emi 764 2942/764 2982/566 7702

The reason for the juxtaposing of these two works seems to have been so that maximum continuity could be ensured when played with the automatic record changer (as was the purpose in all previous automatic coupling issues of the 78rpm records)

157 (238)/25 january 1951/concert recording in vienna konzerthaus

wiener symphoniker/wiener singakademie/irmgard seefried/ dietrich fischer-dieskau

brahms ein deutsches requiem: selig sind die da leid tragen; herr lehre doch mich: wie lieblich sind deine wohnungen; ihr habt nun traurigkeit

lp issue: japan AT 01-02

cd issues: refrain DR 92 0021/japanes furtwängler centre WFHC 023/ orfeo C834 118Y

issues prior to orfeo included the missing movements taken from other performances (not all conducted by furtwängler)

158 (239)/19-20 february 1951/hmv sessions in london abbey road studios/*producer walter legge*

philharmonia orchestra/edwin fischer (piano)

beethoven piano concerto no 5 in e flat op 73 "emperor"

2EA 15407 DB 21315
2EA 15408
2EA 15409 DB 21316
2EA 15412
2EA 15413 DB 21317
2EA 15414
2EA 15415 DB 21318
2EA 15416
2EA 15417 DB 21319
2EA 15421

lp issues: hmv ALP 1051/HLM 7027/FALP 121/FALP 30043/UVT 3034/
QALP 10024/electrola E 90048/WALP 1051/EBE 600 000/STE 90048/
SME 90048/SMVP 8039/columbia (austria) VALP 536/victor LHMV 4/
eterna 820 031/vox turnabout THS 65072/emi 1C027 00803M/
1C045 50023/1C047 00803M/29 00013/29 00021/2C153 52540-52551/
3C153 53800-53805M

cd issues: emi 761 0052/907 8782/naxos 8.112025/
chibas restorations 1144/warner (japan) WPCS 10910

78rpm edition was also published in automatic coupling with the numbers DB 9661-9665

159 (240)/27 february 1951/rias interview recording in berlin hochschule für musik

furtwängler talks to an audience of students

lp issues: deutsche grammophon KL 29-32/004 279/2720 202/
2730 005/2740 260

cd issues: deutsche grammophon 477 0062/audite 21 403

160 (241)/13 april 1951/stage recording in milan teatro alla scala

orchestra e coro del teatro alla scala/fedora barbieri/hilde güden/ magda gabory

gluck orfeo ed euridice

lp issues: unique opera recordings UORC 169/discocorp RR 419/ estro armonico EA 022/cetra LO 19/FE 46/vox turnabout THS 65112-65113

cd issues: documents LV 933-934/walhall WLCD 0076/urania 22 196/ opera dubs OD 10229

walhall edition is incorrectly dated 7 april 1951

161 (244 and 246-247)/19-25 april 1951/concert recordings in cairo and alexandria

philharmonisches orchester berlin

tchaikovsky symphony no 6 in b minor op 64 "pathetique"

lp issues: deutsche grammophon 2535 165/longanesi GCL 23

cd issue: deutsche grammophon 474 0302

wagner parsifal: karfreitagszauber

lp issues: deutsche grammophon 2535 826/2721 202/2740 260

cd issues: deutsche grammophon 415 6632/427 4062/439 8372/474 0302/ music and arts CD 794/archipel ARPCD 0261

bruckner symphony no 7 in e

lp issues: deutsche grammophon 2535 161/2721 202/2740 201/2740 260

cd issues: deutsche grammophon 439 8372/445 4182

It is not certain if other recorded items from this visit to Egypt still survive in radio archives

162 (249-252)/1 may 1951/concert recordings in rome auditorium del foro italico

philharmonisches orchester berlin

bruckner symphony no 7 in e

lp issues: rococo 2105/discocorp RR 416/cetra FE 42/nippon columbia OZ 7601

cd issues: arkadia CDWFE 362/music and arts CD 698/membran 222 128/tahra FURT 1098/myto 00183

debussy nocturnes: nuages et fetes

lp issues: discocorp BWS 708/DIS 708/cetra FE 15

cd issues: cetra CDE 1044/music and arts CD 719/myto 00183

strauss don juan

lp issue: cetra FE 41

cd issue: myto 00183

wagner tannhäuser overture

lp issues: discocorp RR 413/deutsche grammophon 2535 826/ 2740 260

cd issues: 415 6632/427 4062/474 0302/music and arts CD 794/ myto 00183/archipel ARPCD 0261

163 (253)/29 july 1951/ rehearsal recording in bayreuth festspielhaus/*producer walter legge*

orchester und chor der bayreuther festspiele/elisabeth schwarzkopf/elisabeth höngen/hans hopf/otto edelmann

beethoven symphony no 9 in d minor op 125 "choral"

lp issues: hmv ALP 1286-1287/FALP 381-382/FALP 30048-30049/COLH 78-79/ UVT 3048-3049/QALP 10116-10117/electrola E 90115-90116/WALP 1286-1287/ EBE 600 000/STE 90115-90116/SMVP 3048-3049/SME 90115-90116/victor LM 6043/angel 4003/angel seraphim 6068/emi RLS 727/1C147 00811-00812/ 1C149 53432-53439M/2C151 53678-53679/2C153 00811-00812/ 2C153 52540-52551/3C153 00811-00812

cd issues: emi 747 0812/763 6062/769 0812/566 9012/907 8782/ japanese furtwängler centre WFHC 030/chibas restorations 1142/ naxos 8.111060

It was only after the recent discovery of Bavarian Radio's tape of the actual concert (Session no. 164 below) that it was fully realised that Walter Legge had edited together pre-performance sections for this LP version eventually published by HMV in 1955

164/29 july 1951/bayerischer rundfunk concert recording in bayreuth festspielhaus

orchester und chor der bayreuther festspiele/elisabeth schwarzkopf/elisabeth höngen/hans hopf/otto edelmann

beethoven symphony no 9 in d minor op 125 "choral"

cd issues: orfeo C754 081B/japanese furtwängler centre WFHC 013/ chibas restorations 1143

This concert officially inaugurated the re-opened Bayreuth Festival, the only other maestro to have conducted the work in the Festspielhaus having been Richard Strauss in 1933

165 (254)/6 august 1951/stage recording in salzburg felsenreitschule

wiener philharmoniker/chor der wiener staatsoper/irmgard seefried/wilma lipp/edith oravez/anton dermota/erich kunz/ josef greindl/paul schoeffler/peter klein/christel goltz/margherita kenney/sieglinde wagner/hannelore steffek/luise leitner/friedl meusburger/fred liewehr/franz höbling/hans beirer/franz bierbach

mozart die zauberflöte

lp issues: cetra LO 9/FE 19/foyer FO 1028

cd issues: foyer 3CF-2003/priceless D 16603/rodolphe RPC 32527-32530/ virtuoso 269 9192/emi 565 3562

166 (256)/7 august 1951/interview recording in salzburg mozarteum

furtwängler talks about verdi and wagner

lp issues: deutsche grammophon KL 27-32/004 279/2721 202/ 2730 005/2740 260

cd issue: deutsche grammophon 477 0062

167 (255)/7 august 1951/stage recording in salzburg festspielhaus

wiener philharmoniker/chor der wiener staatsoper/ramon vinay/ carla martinis/sieglinde wagner/paul schoeffler/august jaresch/ josef greindl/franz bierbach/georg monthy

verdi otello

lp issues: mrf records MRF 45/discocorp IGI 342/cetra LO 6/FE 28/ vox turnabout THS 65120-65122/foyer FO 1018

cd issues: foyer 2CF-2002/arkadia CDWFE 303/CDWFE 353/rodolphe RPC 32561-32562/virtuoso 269 7382/emi 565 7512

168/15 august 1951/rehearsal recording in lucerne kunsthaus

schweizerisches festspielorchester

beethoven symphony no 7: second movement rehearsal

lp issues: french furtwängler society SWF 7401/japan JPL 1006/ nippon columbia OZ 7597

cd issues: french furtwängler society SWF 961-962/music and arts CD 1018

169 (257-259)/19 august 1951/concert recording in salzburg festspielhaus

wiener philharmoniker/dietrich fischer-dieskau

mendelssohn hebrides overture

lp issues: german furtwängler society F667.497-498/discocorp RR 314/ cetra FE 45/nippon columbia OZ 7590

cd issues: salzburg festival-orfeo SF 001/orfeo 409 048L

mahler lieder eines fahrenden gesellen

lp issues: cetra LO 510/FE 29/rococo 2105/discocorp IGI 382/RR 314/ german furtwängler society F667.497-498.nippon columbia OZ 7603

cd issues: priceless D 18355/cetra CDE 1045/virtuoso 269 7392/ orfeo C409 048L

bruckner symphony no 5 in b flat

lp issues: rococo 2034/discocorp RR 314/RR 508/cetra FE 42/ german furtwängler society F667.497-498

cd issues: virtuoso 269 7342/arkadia CDWFE 360/emi 565 7502/ orfeo C409 048L

Orfeo is the clear recommendation for this complete concert

170 (260)/31 august 1951/concert recording in salzburg festspielhaus

wiener philharmoniker/chor der wiener staatsoper/salzburger domchor/irmgard seefried/sieglinde wagner/anton dermota/ josef greindl

beethoven symphony no 9 in d minor op 125 "choral"

cd issue: orfeo C409 048L

newsreel filmfootage also exists of the concluding bars of the symphony

171 (261)/4 september 1951/sender freies berlin rehearsal recording in berlin schillertheater

philharmonisches orchester berlin

gluck alceste overture

cd issue: german furtwängler society TMK 05294

172 (262)/5 september 1951/rias concert recording in berlin schillertheater

philharmonisches orchester berlin

gluck alceste overture

lp issues: deutsche grammophon 2535 804/cetra FE 50/japan AT 04

cd issues: deutsche grammophon 477 0062/refrain DR 92 0018/ elaborations ELA 903/audite 21 403

japan, refrain and elaborations editions were all incorrectly dated 4 september 1951; tape of beethoven ninth from this concert was erased on the explicit instructions of the condutor

173/22 october 1951/concert recordings in stuttgart liederhalle

wiener philharmoniker

haydn symphony no 88 in g

lp issues: french furtwängler society SWF 8501/victor (japan) RCL 3337

cd issues: virtuoso 269 7332/evangel FRL 1002/french furtwängler society SWF 931

ravel rapsodie espagnole

lp issues: cetra FE 15/french furtwängler society SWF 8501

cd issues: virtuoso 269 7332/french furtwängler society SWF 931/ evangel FRL 1002/music and arts CD 719

bruckner symphony no 4 in e flat "romantic"

lp issues: deutsche grammophon 2740 201/discocorp RR 557

cd issues: deutsche grammophon 415 6642/427 4032/445 4152/japanese furtwängler centre WFHC 018-020

174 (264-265)/27 october 1951/concert recordings in hamburg musikhalle/*sound engineer friedrich schnapp*

sinfonieorchester des nordwestdeutschen rundfunks

brahms haydn variations op 56a

lp issues: french furtwängler society SWF 8201-8202.japan AT 01-02

cd issues: as-disc AS 113/french furtwängler society SWF 881/nuova era 013.6332-6334/music and arts CD 941/tahra FURT 1001

brahms symphony no 1 in c minor op 68

lp issues: french furtwängler society SWF 8201-8202/victor (japan) RCL 3335

cd issues: french furtwangler SWF 881/nuova era 013.6332-6334/ music and arts CD 941/tahra FURT 1001

Either Tahra or French Furtwängler Society can be safely recommended for these two remarkable performances

175 (266-268)/29 october 1951/concert recordings in munich deutsches museum

wiener philharmoniker

beethoven coriolan overture op 62
lp issues: decca ECM 684/592.110
cd issues: nuova era 013.6313/013.6300/elaborations ELA 906/
french furtwängler society SWF 892/orfeo C559 022I

schumann symphony no 1 in b flat op 38 "spring"
lp issues: mrf records MRF 45/MRF 64/decca ECM 684/592.110/417 2871/
nippon columbia DXM 170
cd issues: decca 417 2872/virtuoso 269 7402/arlecchino ARL 151-152/
deutsche grammophon 477 0062/orfeo C559 022I

bruckner symphony no 4 in e flat "romantic"
lp issue: decca ECM 685
cd issues: priceless D 14228/virtuoso 269 7372/music and arts CD 796/
orfeo C559 022I/tahra FURT 1090-1093

176 (270-271)/22 and 27-28 november and 2-4 december 1951/ deutsche grammophon sessions in berlin jesus-christus-kirche

philharmonisches orchester berlin/*producer fred hamel*

furtwängler symphony no 2 in e minor

lp issues: deutsche grammophon LPM 18 017-18 018/LPM 18 114-18 115/ 2707 086/2721 202/japan M 2431-2432

cd issues: deutsche grammophon 439 8372/457 7222

schubert symphony no 9 in c D944 "great"

03142 LVM 72 153
03143
03144 LVM 72 154
03145
03146 LVM 72 155
03147
03148 LVM 72 156
03149

lp issues: deutsche grammophon LPM 18 015-18 016/LPM 18 347/KL 27-32/ 2535 808/2721 202/2730 005/2740 260/heliodor 88 006/eterna 820 068/ decca (usa) DX 119/DL 9746/heliodor (usa) H 25074/HS 25074

cd issues: deutsche grammophon 415 6602/427 4052/439 8322/447 4392/ naxos 8.111344

78rpm edition was on newly developed longer playing discs described as variable grade; LPM 18 347 was published in editions with and without side break in second movement

177 (269)/4-5 december 1951/deutsche grammophon sessions in berlin jesus-christus-kirche/*producer fred hamel*

philharmonisches orchester berlin

haydn symphony no 88 in g

03138	LVM 72 157
03139	
03140	LVM 72 158
03141	

lp issues: deutsche grammophon LPM 18 015/LPM 18 283/LPM 18 725/ LPM 18 858/KL 27-32/478 146/2535 828/2721 202/2730 005/2740 260/ heliodor 88 007/decca (usa) DX 119/DL 9767/heliodor (usa) H 25073

cd issues: deutsche grammophon 415 6612/427 4042/439 8392/ 447 4392/japanese furtwängler centre WFHC 011

78rpm edition was on newly developed longer playing discs described as variable grade

178 (273-275)/december 1951/film and sound recordings made for the film "botschafter der musik" in berlin titania palast

philharmonisches orchester berlin

wagner die meistersinger von nürnberg overture: opening bars; schubert symphony no 8 "unfinished": rehearsal of opening bars; strauss till eulenspiegels lustige streiche

lp issues: period SPL 716/everest SDBR 3252 (meistersinger and till)/ nippon columbia OS 7076 (schubert and till)

cd issue: french furtwängler society SWF 8403-8404 (schubert)

vhs video: teldec 4509 950383/4509 957103 (till)

laserdisc: teldec 4509 950386

the performance of till eulenspiegel includes a filmed ballet sequence; all these extracts are also to be seen in various film documentaries about furtwängler

179 (276-277)/10 january 1952/concert recordings in rome auditorium del foro italico

orchestra sinfonica di roma della rai

beethoven symphony no 6 in f op 68 "pastoral"
lp issues: olympic OL 8120/OL 8128/cetra FE 5
cd issue: myto 00197

beethoven symphony no 5 in c minor op 67
lp issues: olympic OL 8120/OL 8126/cetra FE 7
cd issue: myto 00197

180/14 january 1952/concert recording in rome auditorium del foro italico orchestra sinfonica di roma della rai/ hilde konetzni/günther treptow/otto von rohr

wagner die walküre; act one
lp issue: cetra FE 47
cd issue: music and arts CD 866

181 (278-279)/19 january 1952/concert recordings in rome auditorium del foro italico

orchestra sinfonica di roma dalla rai/pietro scarpini (piano)

beethoven piano concerto no 4 in g op 58
lp issues: discocorp RR 441/cetra FE 2/nippon columbia OZ 7595
cd issues: as-disc AS 373/myto 00202

beethoven symphony no 3 in flat op 55 "eroica"
lp issues: olympic OL 8120/OL 8122/cetra FE 6
cd issues: urania 22 251/myto 00202

182 (280)/27 january 1952/concert recording in vienna schönbrunner schlosstheater

wiener philharmoniker/paul badura-skoda (piano)

mozart piano concerto no 22 in e flat K482

lp issues: discocorp AUDAX 765/french furtwängler socuety SWF 8401-8402/ nippon columbia OZ 7602/OW 7826

cd issues: music and arts CD 895/CD 1097/orfeo C834 118Y/german furtwängler society TMK 200406152

Only Music and Arts CD 1097, Orfeo and German Furtwängler Society present the recording in its original form, all earlier incarnations having been assembled from various inferior sources and performances not conducted by Furtwängler

183 (281-283)/27 january 1952/concert recordings in vienna musikvereinssaal

wiener philharmoniker/willi boskovsky (violin)/emanuel brabec (cello)

brahms haydn variations op 56a

lp issues: emi 1C149 53420-53426M/2C153 53420-53426/ 3C153 53661-53669M

cd issues: testament SBT 1142/orfeo C834 118Y/pristine audio PASC 340

brahms double concerto in a minor op 102

lp issues: cetra FE 16/emi 1C149 53420-53426M/2C153 53420-53426/ 3C153 53661-53669M

cd issues: curcio CDN 05/emi 252 3212/763 4962/orfeo C834 118Y/ pristine audio PASC 341

brahms symphony no 1 in c minor op 68

lp issue: emi ED 29 01241

cd issues: membran 20.3090/20.3094/223 508/emi 252 3212/565 5132/ 907 8782/orfeo C834 118Y/pristine audio PASC 340

emi 252 3212 and membran issues incorrectly dated november 1947

184 (284)/3 february 1952/concert recording in vienna musikvereinssaal

wiener philharmoniker/wiener singakademie/hilde güden/
rosette anday/julius patzak/alfred poell

beethoven symphony no 9 in d minor op 125 "choral"
lp issue: rococo 2109
cd issues: refrain DR 91 0003/orfeo C834 118Y/tahra sacd FURT 2012

185 (285-288)/10 february 1952/sender freies berlin concert recordings in berlin titania palast

philharmonisches orchester berlin

beethoven grosse fuge op 133
lp issues: deutsche grammophon LPM 18 859/2535 813/heliodor 88 023
cd issues: deutsche grammophon 477 0062/german furtwängler society TMK 200601920/pristine audio PASC 370

honegger mouvement symphonique no 3
lp issue: cetra FE 15
cd issues: cetra CDE 1044/virtuoso 269 7322/music and arts CD 719/ german furtwängler society TMK 05294/TMK 200601920/french furtwängler society SWF 001-002

schubert symphony no 8 in b minor D759 "unfinished"
lp issues: deutsche grammophon 2535 804/2721 202
cd issues: deutsche grammophon 423 5722/439 8322/474 0302/ virtuoso 269 7322/german furtwängler society TMK 200601920

brahms symphony no 1 in c minor op 68
lp issues: deutsche grammophon 2535 162/2721 202
cd issues: deutsche grammophon 415 6622/415 4022/439 8322/477 0062/ virtuoso 269 9072/venezia V-1001/japanese furtwängler society WFJ 25-26/ french furtwängler society SWF 062-064/german furtwängler society TMK 200601920

186 (289-291)/3 march 1952/radio recordings in turin
auditorium via montebello

orchestra sinfonica di torino della rai

haydn symphony no 88 in g
lp issues: discocorp RR 399/nippon columbia OS 7075
cd issues: as-disc AS 371/historical performers HP 11

beethoven leonore no 3 overture op 72a
lp issue: cetra FE 48

ravel rapsodie espagnole
lp issues: discocorp BWS 708/DISC 708/nippon columbia OZ 7592

strauss tod und verklärung
cd issue: cetra CDE 1045

187 (292-293)/7 march 1952/concert recordings in turin
sala del conservatorio

orchestra sinfonica di torino della rai/gioconda da vito (violin)

brahms violin concerto in d op 77
lp issues: rococo 2027/discocorp RR 510/nippon columbia DXM 159/
OW 7819/cetra FE 3
cd issues: refrain MADR 204/music and arts CD 804/urania 22 207/
tahra FURT 1080-1081

brahms symphony no 1 in c minor op 68
lp issue: rococo 2017
cd issues: urania 22 224/tahra FURT 1080-1081

188 (294-298)/11 march 1952/concert recordings in turin sala del conservatorio

orchestra sinfonica di torino della rai/gioconda da vito (violin)

schubert rosamunde overture D644
lp issues: discocorp RR 405/cetra FE 50/nippon columbia OZ 7590

schubert symphony no 8 in b minor D759 "unfinished"
lp issues: japan W 19/AT 05-06
cd issues: refrain DR 92 0023/tahra FURT 1080-1081

mendelssohn violin concerto in e minor op 64
lp issues: rococo 2017/discocorp RR 510/nippon columbia DXM 159/ OW 7819/cetra FE 35
cd issues: refrain MADR 204/tahra FURT 1080-1081

wagner tristan und isolde: vorspiel und liebestod
lp issues: cetra LAR 46/FE 43
cd issues: cetra CDE 1012/CDAR 2032/ARCD 2054/urania 22 201/ warner fonit 5050466 296528

189 (299)/9 april 1952/concert recording in vienna konzerthaus

wiener philharmoniker/wiener singakademie/wiener sängerknaben/irmgard seefried/hilde rössel-majdan/ julius patzak/otto wiener/hans braun

bach matthäus-passion BWV 244: part one nos. 1-33 only
lp issue: japan GCL 5003
cd issues: french furtwängler society SWF 061/orfeo C834 118Y

Orfeo confirms that this performance was privately recorded and that it only survives in this fragmentary form

190 (301)/7 may 1952/concert recording in munich deutsches museum

philharmonisches orchester berlin

brahms symphony no 2 in d op 73

lp issues: emi 1C147 50336-50339M/1C149 53420-53426M/1C04901532/ 2C153 53420-53426/3C153 53661-53669M

cd issues: virtuoso 269 9072/emi 252 3212/565 5132/907 8782/french furtwängler society SWF 062-064/pristine audio PASC 341

191 (302)/25-26 may 1952/electrola sessions in berlin jesus-christus-kirche

philharmonisches orcheser berlin/yehudi menuhin (violin)

mendelssohn violin concerto in e minor op 64

45rpm issue: victor WDM 1720

reel-to-reel tape: hmv HTA 2

lp issues: hmv ALP 1135/FALP 312/GHLP 1016/QALP 10071/electrola E 90074/WALP 1135/E 60546/WDLP 602/SME 91486/SMVP 8040/ victor LM 1720/angel (argentina) LPC 11582/emi 1C047 00907/2C051 03612

cd issues: movimento musica 051.052/emi 747 1192/769 7992/ 566 9752/907 8782

192 (303)/31 may 1952/concert recording in rome auditorium del foro italico

orchestra sinfonica e coro di roma della rai/kirsten flagstad/ hilde konetzni/ludwig suthaus/josef hermann/josef greindl/ julia moor/elisabeth lindermeier/ruth michaelis

wagner götterdämmerung: act three

lp issues: ed smith EJS 318/cetra FE 20

cd issue: music and arts CD 866

ed smith edition was incorrectly described as milan 1950

193 (304-307)/6 june 1952/concert recordings in turin
sala del conservatorio

orchestra sinfonica di torino della rai

wagner der fliegende holländer overture
lp issue: cetra FE 47
cd issues: cetra CDE 1012/CDAR 2032/music and arts CD 712/CD 794/
urania 22 224/warner fonit 5050466 296528/archipel ARPCD 0261

wagner siegfried idyll
lp issue: cetra FE 47
cd issues: cetra CDE 1012/CDAR 2032/music and arts CD 712/
urania 22 207/warner fonit 5050466 296528/archipel ARPCD 0261

wagner götterdämmerung: siegfrieds rheinfahrt
lp issue: cetra FE 47
cd issues: cetra CDE 1012/CDAR 2032/warner fonit 5050466 296528/
archipel ARPCD 0261

tchaikovsky symphony no 5 in e minor op 64
lp issues: discocorp DIS 3702/olympic OL 8137/nippon columbia OZ 7591
cd issues: as-disc AS 371/historical performers HP 11/
music and arts CD 712/urania 22 201

194 (308)/10-22 june 1952/hmv sessions in london
kingsway hall/*producer walter legge*

philharmonia orchestra/chorus of the royal opera house/kirsten flagstad/blanche thebom/ludwig suthaus/dietrich fischer-dieskau/ josef greindl/rudolf schock/edgar evans/rhoderick davies

wagner tristan und isolde
lp issues: hmv ALP 1030-1035/RLS 684/HQM 1001-1005/FALP 221-226/
FALP 30331-30335/electrola E 90032-90037/WALP 1030-1035/E 91170-91174/
WALP 574-578/columbia (austria) VALP 521-526/victor LM 6700/angel 3588/
emi 1C147 00899-00903M/10 08993/EX 29 06843
cd issues: emi 747 3228/556 2542/567 6212/907 8782/naxos 8.110321-4

195 (309)/23 june 1952/hmv session in london kingsway hall/ *producer walter legge*

philharmonia orchestra/kirsten flagstad

wagner götterdämmerung: starke scheite schichtet mir dort

lp issues: hmv ALP 1016/HQM 1057/FALP 194/FALP 30295/QALP 10079/ electrola E 90026/WALP 1016/E 80954/WCLP 953/victor LHMV 1072/ emi 1C047 01149M/angel seraphim 60033/melodiya D 033213-033214

cd issue: emi 764 9352

catalogue number FALP 194 was also used for the 1948 recording of this work (session no. 102)

196 (310)/24-25 june 1952/hmv sessions in london kingsway hall/*producer lawrance collingwood*

philharmonia orchestra/dietrich fischer-dieskau

mahler lieder eines fahrenden gesellen

reel-to-reel tape: hmv HTB 409

lp issues: hmv ALP 1270/XLP 30044/FALP 392/FALP 30250/electrola E 90106/WALP 1270/SME 91387/SHZE 338/angel 35522/melodiya D 06441-06442/emi 1C063 00898/100 8981/2C061 01208

cd issue: emi 747 6572

197 (311)/24-25 november 1952/hmv sessions in vienna musikvereinssaal/*producer lawrance collingwood*

wiener philharmoniker

beethoven symphony no 6 in f op 68 "pastoral"

reel-to-reel tape: hmv HTA 5

lp issues: hmv ALP 1041/FALP 288/FALP 30038/UVT 3038/QALP 10034/ electrola E 90040/WALP 1041/SME 90040/SMVP 8038/victor LHMV 1066/ columbia (austria) VALP 535/angel (argentina) LPC 11526/eterna 820 045/ unicorn WFS 9/emi 1C149 53432-53439M/1C027 00807M/100 8071/ 2C153 52540-52551

cd issues: emi 747 1212/763 6062/763 0342/907 8782/pristine audio PASC 359

198 (312-313)/24 and 26-28 november 1952/hmv sessions in vienna musikvereinssaal/*producer lawrance collingwood*

wiener philharmoniker

beethoven symphony no 1 in c op 21

lp issues: hmv ALP 1324/FALP 30124/FBLP 25023/UVT 3124/electrola E 90132/WALP 1324/E 60657/WDLP 663/SME 91412/victor LHMV 700/ melodiya D 03375-03376/emi RLS 727/1C149 53432-53439M/ 1C027 00806M/ 2C153 52540-52551/2C153 53678-53679

cd issues: emi 747 4092/763 6062/763 0332/907 8782

beethoven symphony no 3 in e flat op 55 "eroica"

lp issues: hmv ALP 1060/FALP 287/FALP 50037/UVT 3037/QALP 10030/ electrola E 90050/WALP 1060/EBE 600 000/STE 90050/SME 90050/ SMVP 8041/columbia (austria) VALP 530/victor LHMV 1044/angel seraphim 6018/world records SH 375/emi 1C149 53432-53439M/ 1C027 00810M/3C053 00810/2C153 52540-52551

cd issues: emi 747 4102/763 6062/763 0332/907 8782

199 (314-316)/29-30 november 1952/concert recordings in vienna musikvereinssaal

wiener philharmoniker/alfred poell

beethoven symphony no 1 in c op 21

lp issues: cetra FE 33/german furtwängler society F669.056-057

cd issues: arkadia CD 504/CDHP 504/curcio CON 02/cetra CDE 1013/ nuova era 013.6305/013.6300/virtuoso 269 7162/emblem EF 4003/ music and arts CD 711/CD 942/tahra FURT 1076-1077/opus kura OPK 7027-7028/orfeo C834 118Y

mahler lieder eines fahrenden gesellen

lp issue: cetra FE 29

cd issues: tahra FURT 1076-1077/orfeo C834 118Y/venezia V-1017

beethoven symphony no 3 in e flat op 55 "eroica"

cd issues: nuova era 013.6314/013.6300/virtuoso 269 7182/ tahra FURT 1076-1077/tahra sacd FURT 2011/orfeo C834 118Y/ venezia V-1017

200 (317-318)/1-3 december 1952/hmv sessions in vienna musikvereinssaal/*producer lawrance collingwood*

wiener philharmoniker

beethoven symphony no 4 in b flat op 60
reel-to-reel tape: hmv HTA 20
lp issues: hmv ALP 1059/FALP 116/FALP 30032/FALP 30124/UVT 3124/ QALP 10025/electrola E 90059/WALP 1059/SME 91412/columbia (austria) VALP 518/victor LHMV 1059/emi MFP 2072/1C149 53432-53439M/ 1C027 00806M/2C153 52540-52551
cd issues: emi 747 4092/763 6062/763 1922/907 8782
catalogue number FALP 116 was also used for the 1950 recording of this work (session no. 129)

wagner tannhäuser overture
45rpm issues: hmv 7ERF 154/ERF 17024
reel-to-reel tape: hmv HTA 16
lp issues: hmv ALP 1220/XLP 30082/FALP 289/FALP 362/FALP 30039/ FALP 30215/FBLP 25057/QALP 10088/electrola E 90023/WALP 1220/ E 90097/WALP 534/E 91074/WALP 561/columbia (austria) VALP 538/ angel seraphim 6024/melodiya D 032137-032138/emi 29 12343/ 1C149 01197-01199M
cd issues: historical performers HP 4/emi 252 3282/764 9352/ naxos 8.111348/praga digitals sacd 350107
this recording was also published on a number of unofficial cd editions, on which it was dated 1940 and described as being played by the berlin staatskapelle

201 (319-321)/7 december 1952/sender freies berlin recordings in berlin titania palast

philharmonisches orchester berlin

weber der freischütz pverture
lp issue: cetra FE 50
cd issue: tahra FURT 1026

hindemith die harmonie der welt
unpublished recording

beethoven symphony no 3 in e flat op 55 "eroica"
lp issues: rococo 2050/discocorp RR 520/german furtwängler society F666.848M/japan WFJ 1/nippon columbia OZ 7584/OW 7818
cd issues: refrain DR 93 0065/music and arts CD 520/tahra FURT 1018/ FURT 1060-1062/chibas restorations 1128

202 (322-324)/8 december 1952/rias concert recordings in berlin titania palast

philharmonisches orchester berlin

weber der freischütz overture
lp issues: german furtwängler society F670.027-028/japan AT 04
cd issues: music and arts CD 795/elaborations ELA 903/ tahra FURT 1026/audite 21 403

hindemith die harmonie der welt
lp issues: discocorp RR 438/german furtwängler society F670.027-028
cd issues: music and arts CD 713/japanese furtwängler society WFJ 13-14/ audite 21 403

beethoven symphony no 3 in e flat op 55 "eroica"
lp issue: cetra LO 530
cd issues: rodolphe RPC 32522-32524/RPV 32801/arkadia CDWFE 363/ emblem EF 4001/music and arts CD 869/tahra FURT 1008-1009/ FURT 1054-1057/FURT 2002-2004/chibas restorations 1130/audite 21 403

A magnificent concert captured complete by RIAS (Audite)

203 (325-326)/15 december 1952/rehearsal recordings in frankfurt-am-main sendersaal des hessischen rundfunks

sinfonieorchester des hessischen rundfunks

gluck iphigenie in aulis overture

lp issues: discocorp RR 419/cetra FE 50/nippon columbia OZ 7512

cd issues: refrain DR 92 0022/emblem EF 5004/german furtwängler society TMK 200601921

furtwängler symphony no 2 in e minor

lp issue: cetra FE 36

cd issue: german furtwängler society TMK 200601921

cetra editions of both works incorrectly dated 16 december 1952

204/22 february 1953/concert recordings in vienna musikvereinssaal

wiener philharmoniker

gluck iphigenie in aulis overture

lp issues: japan GMV 10S/AT 09-10

cd issues: refrain DR 92 0022/theatre 400 3531/german furtwängler society TMK 10670/orfeo C834 118Y

furtwängler symphony no 2 in e minor

cd issues: theatre 400 3531/orfeo C375 941B/C834 118Y

205 (327-329)/7-9 april 1953/hmv sessions in london kingsway hall/

producers lawrance collingwood and david bicknell

philharmonia orchestra/yehudi menuhin (violin)

beethoven violin concerto in d op 61

lp issues: hmv ALP 1100/FALP 314/FALP 30041/UVT 3041/QALP 10056/ electrola E 90065/WALP 1100/EBE 600 000/STE 90065/SME 90065/ SMVP 8050/columbia (austria) VALP 537/eterna 820 547/victor LHMV 1061/angel seraphim 60135/emi 1C047 00117M/ 2C153 52540-52551/3C153 53800-53805M

cd issues: movimento musica 051.052/emi 747 1192/769 7992/566 9752/ chibas restorations 1144

beethoven violin romances nos 1 in g op 40 and 2 in f op 50

45rpm issues: hmv E 41131 (no 1)/E 41686 (no 2)/E 50513/7ERW 5371/ 7EGW 8597 (no 1)/7EGW 8751

reel-to-reel tape: hmv HTA 2

lp issues: hmv ALP 1135/HLM 7015/FALP 312/FBLP 25051/QALP 10071/ electrola E 90074/WALP 1135/angel seraphim 60135 (no 1)/angel (argentina) LPC 11582/emi 2C153 52540-52551/3C153 53800-53805M

cd issue: testament SBT 1109

206 (330-333)/14 april 1953/sender freies berlin recordings in berlin titania palast

philharmonisches orchester berlin

beethoven symphony no 8 in f op 93
lp issues: german furtwängler society F666.624-625/discocorp RR 413/ japan WFJ 2-3/cetra FE 48/nippon columbia OZ 7585
cd issues: rodolphe RPC 32522-32524/music and arts CD 942/ deutsche grammophon 415 6662/427 4012/477 0062/tahra FURT 2002-2004/ japanese furtwängler society WFJ 24/german furtwängler society TMK 014128/pristine audio PASC 359

strauss till eulenspiegels lustige streiche
lp issues: german furtwängler society F666.624-625/japan WFJ 2-3
cd issues: nuova era 013.6317/virtuoso 269 7302/evangel FRL 1003/ german furtwängler society TMK 014128

interval interview: wilhelm furtwängler talks to dr erwin kroll
lp issues: german furtwängler society F666.624-625/japan WFJ 2-3
cd issue: german furtwängler society TMK 014128

beethoven symphony no 7 in a op 92
lp issues: german furtwängler society F666.624-625/japan WFJ 2-3/ discocorp RR 476/cetra FE 4
cd issues: rodolphe RPC 32422-32424/music and arts CD 942/ deutsche grammophon 415 6662/427 4012/474 0302/ german furtwängler society TMK 014128/tahra FURT 2002-2004

German Furtwängler Society is clearly recommended for giving us the complete concert including the interval discussion

207/16 april 1953/rehearsal and rehearsal performance recordings in hamburg musikhalle

philharmonisches orchester berlin

ravel valses nobles et sentimentales

lp issue: japan GMV 10S

cd issue: tahra FURT 1014-1015

208/28-30 april 1953/interview recording in paris

furtwängler speaks in french to f. goldbeck

cd issue: fench furtwängler society SWF 942-943

209 (334)/14 may 1953/deutsche grammophon session in berlin jesus-christus-kirche/*producer wolfgang lohse*

philharmonisches orchester berlin

schumann symphony no 4 in d minor op 120

04866	LVM 72 361
04867	
04868	LVM 72 362
04869	
04870	LVM 72 363

lp issues: deutsche grammophon LP 16 063/LPE 17 170/LPM 18 858/ KL 27-32/478 146/2535 805/2721 202/2730 005/2740 260/heliodor 88 008/decca (usa) DL 9767/heliodor (usa) H 25073/HS 25073/ longanesi GCL 15

cd issues: arlecchino ARL 151-152/deutsche grammophon 415 6612/ 427 4042/439 8322/457 7222/japanese furtwängler centre WFHC 011/ tahra FURT 1099-1100

78rpm edition was on newly developed longer playing discs described as variable grade

210 (335-337)/18 may 1953/sender freies berlin recordings in berlin titania palast

philharmonisches orchester berlin/wolfgang schneiderhan (violin)

stravinsky le baiser de la fee
lp issues: discococorp DIS 708/BWS 708/cetra FE 14/nippon columbia OZ 7592
german furtwänger socuety F668.164-165M
cd issues: cetra CDE 1043/virtuoso 269 7392/music and arts CD 713/
german furtwängler society TMK 014128/tahra FURT 1019/
japanese furtwängler society WFJ 33-34

beethoven violin concerto in d op 61
lp issues: deutsche grammophon LPM 18 855/KL 27-32/2535 809/
2730 005/heliodor 88 024
cd issues: amadeo 431 3452/431 3432/deutsche grammophon 474 7282/
japanese furtwängler society WFJ 33-34/pristine audio PASC 370

brahms symphony no 1 in c minor op 68
lp issues: discocorp RR 418/everest SDBR 3437/cetra FE 13/
nippon columbia 7820
cd issues: elaborations ELA 902/german furtwängler society TMK 05298/
tahra FURT 1019/japanese furtwängler society WFJ 33-34

211/30 may 1953/concert recording in vienna musikvereinssaal

wiener philharmonikee/wiener singakademie/irngard seefried/
rosette anday/anton dermota/paul schoeffler

beethoven symphony no 9 in d minor oo 125 "choral"
cd issues: ica classics ICAC 5034/japanese furtwängler centre WFHC 025-026

212/31 may 1953/concert recording in vienna musikvereinssaal

wiener philharmoniker/wiener singakademie/irmgard seefried/ rosette anday/anton dermota/paul schoeffler

beethoven symphony no 9 in d minor op 125 "choral"

lp issues: discocorp RR 460/german furtwängler society F669.056-057/ nippon columbia OZ 7588

cd issues: rodolphe RPC 32465/arkadia CD 532/CDHP 532/nuova era 013.6301/013.6300/virtuoso 269 7202/music and arts CD 942/ deutsche grammophon 435 3252/435 3212/orfeo C834 118Y/ japanese furtwängler centre WFHC 025-026

some editions were incorrectly dated and named incorrect vocal soloists

213 (338)/27 july 1953/stage recording in salzburg felsenreitschule

wiener philharmoniker/chor der wiener staatsoper/elisabeth schwarzkopf/elisabeth grümmer/erna berger/anton dermota/ cesare siepi/otto edelmann/walter berry/raffaele arie

mozart don giovanni

lp issues: morgan MOR 003/cetra FE 23

cd issues: rodolphe RPC 32527-32530//virtuoso 269 9052/gala 100 602/ cetra CDE 1050/arkadia CD 509/laudis 4001/orfeo C624 043/music and arts CD 1129/line 500469/archipel ARPCD 0162/french furtwängler society SWF 121-123

opening radio announcement for this performance can be heard on japanese furtwängler society WFJ 25-26

It appears that Archipel has had access to a much better quality source for their edition, although the claim that it is a stereo recording may be excessive

214 (339)/11 august 1953/stage recording in salzburg festspielhaus

wiener philharmoniker/chor der wiener staatsoper/elisabeth schwarzkopf/irmgard seefried/hilde güden/paul schoeffler/ erich kunz/sieglinde wagner/liselotte maikl/peter klein/ erich majkut/endre koreh/alois pernserstorfer

mozart le nozze di figaro/*sung in german*

lp issues: great mozart recordings GMR 999/cetra LO 8/FE 27/ discocorp IGI 343

cd issues: rodolphe RPC 32527-32530/eklipse EKR 59/archipel ARPCD 0163/emi 566 0802

The best recommendation here is EMI; it has sometimes been suggested that the perfomance on Great Mozart Recordings GMR 999 was taken from the performance on 7 August 1953

215 (340-361)/12 august 1953/concert recording in salzburg mozarteum

elisabeth schwarzkopf/wilhelm furtwängler (piano)

hugo wolf liederabend: im frühling; elfenlied; lebewohl; schlafendes jesuskind; phänomen; die spröde; die bekehrte; anakreons grab; blumengruss; epiphanias; wie lange schon; was soll der zorn?; nein junger herr; mein liebster hat zu tische; bedeckt mich mit blumen; herr was trägt der boden hier?; in dem schatten meiner locken; mögen alle bösen zungen; wie glänzt der helle mond; wiegenlied im sommer; nachtzauber; die zigeunerin

lp issues: cetra FE 30/emi 143 5491

cd issues: cetra CDC 21/virtuoso 269 7312/emi 567 5702

prior to publication of the complete recital, the following editions offered selections from the material:

lp issues: emi ALP 2114/1C063 01915M/angel seraphim 60179/ discocorp IGI 382/RR 208/melodram MEL 088

cd issues: virtuoso 269 7152/priceless D 18355/orfeo C826 103D

216/26 august 1953/concert recordings in lucerne kunsthaus

schweizerisches festspielorchester

schumann symphony no 4 in d minor op 120; beethoven symphony no 3 in e flat op 55 "eroica"

cd issues: french furtwängler society SWF 961-962/elaborations ELA 904-905/music and arts CD 1018

217 (362-363)/30 august 1953/concert recordings in salzburg festspielhaus

wiener philharmoniker

hindemith die harmonie der welt

lp issue: cetra FE 22

cd issues: cetra CDE 1049/emi 565 3532/orfeo C409 048L

schubert symphony no 9 in c D944 "great"

lp issue: victor (japan) RCL 3336

cd issues: virtuoso 269 7362/emi 565 3532/orfeo C409 048L/ tahra FURT 1095-1097

Strauss Don Juan was the opening work in this concert, but as the recording is unavailable at source, both emi and orfeo have substituted the 1954 hmv studio version (session no. 236)

218 (364-365)/4 september 1953/concert recordings in munich deutsches museum

wiener philharmoniker

beethoven egmont overture op 84

lp issues: cetra FE 50/japan AT 04/AT 07-08

cd issues: rodolphe RPC 32522-32524/french furtwängler society SWF 892/ melodram MEL 25009/elaborations ELA 906/music and arts CD 792/ tahra FURT 1090-1093

AT 04 and CDM 25009 incorrectly dated this as 24 september 1948

beethoven symphony no 4 in b flat op 60

lp issues: cetra FE 49/victor (japan) RCL 3333

cd issues: nuova era 013.6310/013.6300/rodolphe RPC 32522-32524/ virtuoso 269 7192/french furtwängler society SWF 892/emblem EF 4005-4006/ music and arts CD 792/CD 942/tahra FURT 1090-1093

beethoven symphony no 3 in e flat op 55 "eroica"

cd issue: emi 562 8752

219 (366)/12-13 september 1953/hmv sessions in london abbey road studios/*producers lawrance collingwood and david bicknell*

philharmonia orchestra/yehudi menuhin (violin)

bartok violin concerto no 2

lp issues: hmv ALP 1121/FALP 313/FALP 30528/electrola E 90070/ WALP 1121/victor LHMV 3/angel (argentina) LPC 11593/ emi 1C053 01322/2C051 01322/2C053 01322

cd issues: priceless D 15100/emi 769 8042/907 8782

220 (367-369)/15 september 1953/rias concert recordings in berlin titania palast

philharmonisches orchester berlin

schubert rosamunde overture D644
lp issues: deutsche grammophon 2535 804/cetra FE 11
cd issues: arkadia CD 525/CDHP 525/virtuoso 269 7362/deutsche grammophon 415 6602/427 4052/477 0062/audite 21 403

schubert symphony no 8 in b minor D759 "unfinished"
lp issues: paragon DSV 52101/cetra FE 11/victor (japan) RCL 3337
cd issues: curcio CON 03/music and arts CD 795/tahra FURT 1017/ japanese furtwängler society WFJ 24/venezia V-1001/audie 21 403

schubert symphony no 9 in c D944 "great"
lp issues: cetra FE 12/german furtwängler society F670.207-208/ longanesi GCL 43
cd issues: arkadia CD 525/CDHP 525/foyer CDS 16005/emblem EF 4002/ music and arts CD 795/tahra FURT 1008-1011/FURT 1017/audite 21 403

Yet another splendid concert presented by Audite in its entirety

221/12 october 1953/stage recording in vienna theater an der wien

orchester und chor der wiener staatsoper/martha mödl/ sena jurinac/wolfgang windgassen/rudolf schock/gottlob frick/ otto edelmann/alfred poell/hermann gallos/franz bierbach

beethoven fidelio
lp issues: replica RPL 2439-2431/cetra FE 8-10
cd issues: cetra CDC 12/priceless D 20902/rodolphe RPC 32494/ virtuoso 269 7272/andante 3090/premiere 1160/archipel ARPCD 0181/ japanese furtwängler centre WFHC 028-029/chibas restorations 1137-1139

Archipel is the highly recommended edition for this top quality recording

222 (370)/13-17 october 1953/hmv sessions in vienna musikvereinssaal/ *producer lawrance collingwood*

wiener philharmoniker/chor der wiener staatsoper/martha mödl/ sena jurinac/wolfgang windgassen/rudolf schock/gottlob frick/ otto edelmann/alfred poell/alwin hendricks/franz bierbach

beethoven fidelio

lp issues: hmv ALP 1130-1132/HQM 1109-1110/FALP 323-325/ QALP 10061-10063/electrola E 90071-90073/WALP 1130-1132/ victor LHMV 700/angel seraphim 6022/emi 1C147 01105-01107M/ 2C153 01105-01107/2C153 52540-52552M

cd issues: emi 764 4962/907 8782/pristine audio PACO 095

Although this recording is generally considered less successful than Furtwängler's various live versions of the opera, it does contain a truly overwhelming performance of the Leonore No 3 Overture (omitted from HQM 1109-1110 and Seraphim 6022) which must be heard, to no better effect than on CD from Pristine Audio PASC 355

223 (371)/26 october 1953/concert recording in rome auditorium del foro italico

orchestra sinfonica di roma della rai/ferdinand frantz/ira malaniuk/ elisabeth grümmer/rut siewert/alfred poell/lorenz fehenberger/ wolfgang windgassen/julius patzak/josef greindl/gottlob frick/ gustav neidlinger/sena jurinac/magda gabory/hilde rössel-majdan

wagner das rheingold

lp issues: mrf records MRF 14/emi RLS 702/RLS 703/29 06703/ 1C147 02275-02277M/angel seraphim 6168

cd issues: emi 767 1242/767 1232/gebhardt JGCD 0060/pristine audio

dvd audio issue: japanese furtwängler centre WFHC 004

224 (372)/29 october 1953/concert recording in rome auditorium del foro italico

orchestra sinfonica di roma della rai/hilde konetzni/
wolfgang windgassen/gottlob frick

wagner die walküre: act one

lp issues: mrf records MRF 41/emi RLS 702/29 06703/
1C147 02278-02282M/angel seraphim 6168

cd issues: arkadia CDWFE 359/emi 767 1272/767 1232/
gebhardt JGCD 0060/pristine audio

225 (372)/3 november 1953/concert recording in rome auditorium del foro italico

orchestra sinfonica di roma della rai/martha mödl/elsa cavelti/
hilde konetzni/wolfgang windgassen/ferdinand frantz/gottlob frick

wagner die walküre: act two

lp issues: mrf records MRF 41/emi RLS 702/29 06703/
1C147 02278-02282M/angel seraphim 6168

cd issues: arkadia CDWFE 359/emi 767 1272/767 1232/
gebhardt JGCD 0060/pristine audio

226 (372)/6 november 1953/concert recording in rome auditorium del foro italico

orchestra sinfonica di roma della rai/martha mödl/hilde konetzni/
ferdinand frantz/judith hellwig/magda gabory/gerda scheyrer/
dagmar schmedes/olga bennings/ira malaniuk/elsa cavelti/
hilde rössel-majdan

wagner die walküre: act three

lp issues: mrf records MRF 41/emi RLS 702/29 06703/
1C147 02278-02282M/angel seraphim 6168

cd issues: arkadia CDWFE 359/emi 767 1272/767 1232/
gebhardt JGCD 0060/pristine audio

227 (373)/10 november 1953/concert recording in rome auditorium del foro italico

orchestra sinfonica di roma della rai/ludwig suthaus/ julius patzak/ferdinand frantz

wagner siegfried: act one

lp issues: mrf records MRF 23/emi RLS 702/29 06703/ 1C147 02283-02288M/angel seraphim 6168

cd issues: arkadia CDWFE 359/emi 767 1312/767 1232/ gebhardt JGCD 0060/pristine audio

228 (373)/13 november 1953/concert recording in rome auditorium del foro italico

orchestra sinfonica di roma dalla rai/ludwig suthaus/ julius patzak/ferdinand frantz/rita streich/ alois pernerstorfer/josef greindl

wagner siegfried: act two

lp issues: mrf records MRF 23/emi RLS 702/29 06703/ 1C147 02283-02288M/angel seraphim 6168

cd issues: arkadia CDWFE 359/emi 767 1312/767 1232/ gebhardt JGCD 0060/pristine audio

229 (373)/17 november 1953/concert recording in rome auditorium del foro italico

orchestra sinfonica di roma della rai/martha mödl/ margarete klose/ludwig suthaus/ferdinand frantz

wagner siegfried: act three

lp issues: mrf records MRF 23/emi RLS 702/29 06703/ 1C147 02283-02288M/angel seraphim 6168

cd issues: arkadia CDWFE 359/emi 767 1312/767 1232/ gebhardt JGCD 0060/pristine audio

230 (374)/20 november 1953/concert recording in rome auditorium del foro italico

orchestra sinfonica di roma della rai/martha mödl/ sena jurinac/margarete klose/ludwig suthaus/alfred poell/josef greindl/hilde rössel-majdan

wagner götterdämmerung: prologue and act one

lp issues: mrf records MRF 34/emi RLS 702/29 06793/ 1C147 02288-02292M/angel seraphim 6168

cd issues: arkadia CDWFE 359/emi 767 1362/767 1232/ gebhardt JGCD 0060/pristine audio

231 (374)/24 november 1953/concert recording in rome auditorium del foro italico

coro e orchestra sinfonica di roma della rai/martha mödl/ sena jurinac/ludwig suthaus/alfred poell/josef greindl/ alois pernerstorfer

wagner götterdämmerung: act two

lp issues: mrf records MRF 34/emi RLS 702/29 06703/ 1C147 02288-02292M/angel seraphim 6168

cd issues: arkadia CDWFE 359/emi 767 1362/767 1232/ gebhardt JGCD 0060/pristine audio

232 (374)/27 november 1953/concert recording in rome auditorium del foro italico

coro e orchestra sinfonica di roma della rai/martha mödl/ sena jurinac/ludwig suthaus/alfred poell/josef greindl/ magda gabory/hilde rössel-majdan

wagner götterdämmerung: act three

lp issues: mrf records MRF 34/emi RLS 702/29 06703/ 1C147 01188-02292M/angel seraphim 6168

cd issues: arkadia CDWFE 359/emi 767 1362/767 1232/ gebhardt JGCD 0060/pristine audio

233/27 november 1953/interview recording in rome auditorium del foro italico

furtwängler speaks in italian about his earliest years as a conductor

lp issue: japan AT 13-14

cd issue: tahra FURT 1041-1042

234 (375)/14-15 december 1953/decca sessions in vienna musikvereinssaal

wiener philharmoniker

franck symphony in d minor

VAR 409 unpublished

VAR 410

VAR 411 unpublished

VAR 412

VAR 413 unpublished

VAR 414

VAR 415 unpublished

VAR 416

VAR 417 unpublished

VAR 418

lp issues: decca LXT 2905/ACL 179/ECS 563/220.037/592.107/417 2871/london (usa) LL 967/CM 9091/R 23027/melodiya D 021093-021094/eurodisc KK 70368/nippon columbia DXM 113

cd issues: decca 417 2872/476 2733/arlecchino ARL 140

melodiya catalogue number was also used for the 1945 recording of this work (session no. 082); DXM 113 was also incorrectly described as the 1945 recording

235 (376)/28 february-1 march 1954/hmv sessions in vienna musikvereinssaal/*producer lawrance collingwood*

wiener philharmoniker

beethoven symphony no 5 in c minor op 67

reel-to-reel tape: hmv HTA 12

lp issues: hmv ALP 1195/FALP 260/FALP 30128/UVT 3128/QALP 10086/ electrola E 90088/WALP 1195/EBE 600 000/STE 90088/SME 90088/ SMVP 8049/victor LHMV 9/eterna 820 053/angel seraphim 6018/ emi 1C027 00771M/1C149 53432-53439M/2C153 52540-52551

cd issues: emi 747 8032/763 6062/769 8032/907 8782

236 (377-380)/2-3 march 1954/hmv sessions in vienna musikvereinssaal/*producer lawrance collingwood*

wiener philharmoniker

wagner götterdämmerung: siegfrieds trauermusik

lp issues: hmv ALP 1016/XLP 30082/FALP 194/FALP 30295/FBLP 25057/ QALP 10079/electrola E 90026/WALP 1016/angel seraphim 60003/ french furtwängler society SWF 8001/emi F666.701/29 12343/ 1C149 01197-01199M

cd issues: emi 252 3582/764 9352/naxos 8.111348/praga digitals sacd 350107

SWF 8001 was incorrectly dated february 1949; catalogue number FALP 194 was also used for the 1950 recording of this work (session no.115)

strauss don juan; till eulenspiegels lustige streiche

reel-to-reel tape: hmv HTB 403

lp issues: hmv ALP 1208/HQM 1137/FBLP 25082/QALP 10085/electrola E 90093/WALP 1208/E 70429/WBLP 561/HZEL 71/victor LHMV 19/angel seraphim 60094/emi 1C049 01155M/10 11551/F666.702

cd issues: emi 764 2942 (don juan)/764 2982 (don juan)/565 3532 (don juan)/ 565 1972/562 7902/907 8782/praga digitals sacd 350100

liszt les preludes

reel-to-reel tape: hmv HTA 16

lp issues: hmv ALP 1220/XLP 30106/FALP 363/FBLP 25024/QALP 10088/ electrola E 90097/WALP 1220/E 60661/WDLP 667/E 80801/WCLP 854/ SME 80801/HZE 105/SHZE 105/emi F666.702/2C053 01193/ 1C149 03584-03586M

cd issues: palladio PD 4122/historical performers HP 14/ emi 565 7702/907 8782

237 (381-383)/4-6 march 1954/hmv sessions in vienna musikvereinssaal/*producer lawrance collingwood*

wiener philharmoniker

wagner lohengrin prelude
reel-to-reel tape: hmv HTA 16
lp issues: hmv ALP 1220/XLP 30082/FALP 362/FALP 30213/QALP 10088/ electrola E 90097/WALP 1220/E 91074/WALP 561/angel seraphim 6024/ melodiya D 032137-032138/emi 29 12343/1C149 01197-01199M
cd issues: historical performers HP 4/emi 252 3282/764 9352/ naxos 8.111348/praga digitals sacd 350107

weber der freischütz overture; euryanthe overture
lp issues: victor LHMV 19/emi XLP 30090/1C149 03584-03586M/ F666.699 (euryanthe)
cd issues: palladio PD 4124/historical performers HP 8/emi 566 7702

238 (384-386)/8 march 1954/hmv session in vienna musikvereinssaal/*producer lawrance collingwood*

wiener philharmoniker

gluck alceste overture; iphigenie in aulis overture
lp issues: emi XLP 30090/1C149 03584-03586M/japan NA 96/ french furtwängler society XPMX 2273
cd issue: emi 566 7702

wagner götterdämmerung: siegfrieds rheinfahrt
lp issues: hmv ALP 1016/XLP 30082/FALP 194/FALP 30295/QALP 10079/ electrola E 90026/WALP 1016/angel seraphim 60003/melodiya D 033213-033214/emi F666.701/1C149 01197-01199M/29 12343
cd issues: emi 252 3282/764 9352/naxos 8.111348/praga digitals sacd 350107
29 12343 and 1C149 01197-01199M were incorrectly dated february 1949; catalogue number FALP 194 was also used for 1949 recording of the work (session no. 115)

239 (387-390)/19-21 march 1954/concert recordings in caracas amfiteatro jose angel lamas

orquesta sinfonica de venezuela

handel concerto grosso in d minor op 6 no 10
lp issue: british furtwängler society FURT 101
cd issues: classical society CSCD 116/archipel ARPCD 0177/chibas restorations

strauss don juan; brahms symphony no 1 in c minor op 68
lp issue: british furtwängler society FURT 101
cd issues: british furtwängler society FURT 102/archipel ARPCD 0177/ chibas restorations

wagner tannhäuser overture
lp issue: japan AT 09-10
cd issues: british furtwängler society FURT 102

240 (391-392)/30 march 1954/sdr recordings in stuttgart-degerloch strassenbahnerwaldheim

sinfonieorchester des süddeutschen rundfunks

furtwängler symphony no 2 in e minor
lp issue: french furtwängler society SWF 8301-8302
cd issue: mediaphon-sdr JA 75.100

beethoven symphony no 1 in c op 21
lp issues: discocorp RR 511/nippon columbia OZ 7587/ french furtwängler society SWF 8301-8302
cd issues: french furtwängler society SWF 931/evangel FRL 1002/ mediaphon-sdr JA 75.100

furtwängler talks with hans müller-kray about his work as a composer
lp issues: french furtwängler society SWF 8501/japan W 28-29
cd issue: timpani 1C-1001

241 (393)/4-5 april 1954/hmv sessions in berlin hochschule für musik/*producer fritz ganss*

philharmonisches orchester berlin

beethoven leonore no 2 overture op 72

lp issues: hmv ALP 1324/electrola E 90132/WALP 1324/E 70362/ WBLP 546/E 70421/WBLP 563/unicorn WFS 4/emi 1C047 00843M/ 1C149 53432-53439M/2C153 52540-52551/3C153 53800-53805M

cd issues: emi 565 5132/907 8782

242/10 april 1954/concert recording in vienna musikvereinssaal

wiener philharmoniker

bruckner symphony no 8 in c minor

lp issue: cetra FE 17

cd issues: arkadia CDWFE 355/emblem EF 4005-4006/orfeo C834 118Y/ japanese furtwängler centre WFHC 27/opus kura OPK 7027-7028

243 (394)/15 april 1954/concert recording in vienna musikvereinssaal

wiener philharmoniker/wiener singakademie/wiener sängerknaben/elisabeth grümmer/marga höffgen/anton dermota/otto edelmann/dietrich fischer-dieskau

bach matthäus-passion BWV 244

lp issues: cetra LO 508/FE 34/movimento musica 03.008

cd issues: movimento musica 013.005/priceless D 20899/virtuoso 269 9212/emi 565 5092/orfeo C834 118Y

Only Orfeo gives us the complete performance, all previous editions (including EMI's "official" one) having been taken from a heavily abridged tape

244 (395-400)/27 april 1954/rias concert recordings in berlin titania palast

philharmonisches orchester berlin

handel concerto grosso in d op 6 no 5

lp issues: deutsche grammophon 2535 806/japan P 1001

cd issues: virtuoso 269 7392/deutsche grammophon 477 5238/ audite 21 403

brahms symphony no 3 in f op 90

lp issues: deutsche grammophon 2535 163/longanesi GCL 05

cd issues: deutsche grammophon 423 5722/477 0062/audite 21 403/ music and arts CD 941/french furtwängler society SWF 062-064/ pristine audio PASC 342

blacher concertante musik

lp issue: cetra FE 26

cd issues: as-disc AS 370/audite 21 403

wagner tristan und isolde: vorspiel und liebestod

lp issues: cetra FE 25/german furtwängler society F666.164-165M/ discocorp RR 229

cd issues: deutsche grammophon 415 6632/427 4062/474 0302/ audite 21 403

Yet another complete concert experience from Audite

245 (401-404)/4 may 1954/concert recordings in paris theatre de l'opera

philharmonisches orchester berlin

weber euryanthe overture
lp issues: deutsche grammmophon 2535 805/cetra LO 519/FE 45
cd issues: french furtwängler society SWF 942-943/ deutsche grammophon 477 0062/tahra FURT 1023-1024/ japanese furtwängler society WFJ 42-43

brahms haydn variations op 56a
lp issues: cetra LO 519/FE 45
cd issues: curcio CON 14/french furtwängler society SWF 942-943/ elaborations ELA 902/tahra FURT 1023-1024/japanese furtwängler society WFJ 42-43

schubert symphony no 8 in b minor D759 "unfinished"
lp issues: cetra LO 519/FE 45/japan TPR 1159/discocorp RR 394/ nippon columbia OZ 7512/OW 7590/OW 7819
cd issues: elaborations ELA 901/french furtwängler society SWF 942-943/tahra FURT 1023-1024/japanese furtwängler society WFJ 42-43

beethoven symphony no 5 in c minor op 67
lp issues: cetra LO 519/FE 45/discocorp RR 522
cd issues: elaborations ELA 901/french furtwängler society SWF 942-943/tahra FURT 1023-1024/japanese furtwängler society WFJ 42-43

This was one of the first Furtwängler concerts to circulate in its entirety, first on LPs from Cetra and now on CD from the French Furtwängler Society and Tahra

246 (405-409)/14 may 1954/concert recordings in turin
sala del conservatorio

philharmonisches orchester berlin

weber euryanthe overture
lp issues: discocorp RR 413/rococo 2106/paragon DSV 52101/
cetra FE 50/nippon columbia OZ 7590
cd issues: as-disc AS 373/tahra FURT 1041-1042

brahms symphony no 3 in f op 90
lp issues: discocorp RR 418/paragon DSV 52101/nippon columbia OW 7822
cd issues: nuova era 013.6332-6334/tahra FURT 1042-1043

strauss till eulenspiegels lustige streiche
lp issue: japan AT 13-14
cd issue: tahra FURT 1042-1043

wagner tristan und isolde: vorspiel und liebestod
lp issue: japan AT 09-10
cd issues: refrain DR 92 0031/tahra FURT 1042-1043

247 (410-412)/15 may 1954/concert recordings in lugano
teatro apollo

philharmonisches orchester berlin/yvonne lefebure (piano)

beethoven symphony no 6 in f op 68 "pastoral"
lp issues: cetra LO 529/discocorp RR 477
cd issue: ermitage ERM 120

mozart piano concerto no 20 in d minor K466
lp issues: french furtwängler society XPMX 2273/unicorn WFS 11/
cetra LO 529/FE 18/discocorp RR 395
cd issues: virtuoso 269 7352/cetra CDE 1015/CDE 3009/as-disc AS 372/
ermitage ERM 120/emi 569 4732/warner (japan) WPCS 12910

strauss till eulenspiegels lustige streiche
lp issues: cetra LO 529/FE 41
cd issues: refrain DR 92 0031/tahra FURT 1008-1011

248 (413-414)/23 may 1954/rias concert recordings in berlin titania palast

philharmonisches orchester berlin

beethoven symphony no 6 in f op 68 "pastoral"

lp issues: german furtwängler society F669.310-311/japan TPR 1159/GHE 86125

cd issues: arkadia CD 504/CDHP 504/nuova era 013.6303/013.6300/virtuoso 269 7162/emblem EF 4004/music and arts CD 869/tahra FURT 1008-1009/ FURT 1054-1057/chibas restorations 1127/audite 21 403

beethoven symphony no 5 in c minor op 67

lp issue: german furtwängler society F669.310-311

cd issues: nuova era 013.6305/013.6300/virtuoso 269 7192/emblem EF 4003/ music and arts CD 869/tahra FURT 1008-1009/FURT 1032-1033/ FURT 1054-1057/chibas restorations 1127/audite 21 403

Chibas Restorations stands out as probably the best of several good transfers of this concert

249 (415)/26 july 1954/stage recording in salzburg festspielhaus

wiener philharmoniker/chor der wiener staatsoper/elisabeth grümmer/rita streich/hans hopf/oskar czerwenka/kurt böhme/ alfred poell/otto edelmann/karl dönch

weber der freischütz

lp issues: discocorp IGS 008-010/IGI 338/cetra LO 21/FE 24/vox turnabout THS 65148-65150/robin hood records RHR 522/hope records HOPE 207/ nippon columbia OZ 7575-7577

cd issues: rodolphe RPC 32519-32520/nuova era 013.6324-6326/ arkadia CDWFE 302/CDWFE 352/virtuoso 269 7222/gala 100 510/ music and arts CD 1064/emi 567 4192/walhall WLCD 0073/tahra FURT 1095-1097

250 (416)/26 july 1954/interview recording in salzburg

furtwängler talks about der freischütz

lp issues: deutsche grammophon KL 27-32/2721 202/2730 005/ 2740 260/japan M1-2433

cd issues: deutsche grammophon 477 0062/german furtwängler society TMK 10670/orfeo SF 012

251 (417)/3 august 1954/stage recording in salzburg felsenreitschule

wiener philharmoniker/chor der wiener staatsoper/elisabeth schwarzkopf/elisabeth grümmer/erna berger/anton dermota/ cesare siepi/otto edelmann/deszö ernster/walter berry

mozart don giovanni

lp issues: morgan records 5302/discocorp MORG 003/cetra LO 7/ nippon columbia OZ 7568-7571/foyer FO 1017/emi 29 06673

cd issues: music and arts CD 003/cetra CDE 1050/arkadia CD 509/ CDHP 509/emi 763 8602

arkadia issues were incorrectly dated 1953; some editions also had the final scene of the opera taken from the 1953 recording (session no, 212)

252 (418)/8 august 1954/rehearsal recording in bayreuth festspielhaus

chor und orchester der bayreuther festspiele/gre brouwenstijn/ ira malaniuk/wolfgang windgassen/ludwig weber

beethoven symphony no 9: third and fourth movements

lp issue: japan AT 07-08

cd issues: refrain DR 92 0033/japanese furtwängler centre WFHC 001-002/ venezia V-1024

253 (419)/9 august 1954/bayerischer rundfunk concert recording in bayreuth festspielhaus

chor und orchester der bayreuther festspiele/gre brouwenstijn/ ira malaniuk/wolfgang windgassen/ludwig weber

beethoven symphony no 9 in d minor op 125 "choral"

lp issue: japan W 16

cd issues: refrain DR 91 0016/music and arts CD 1017/japanese furtwängler centre WFHC 001-002

254 (420)/22 august 1954/concert recording in lucerne kunsthaus

philharmonia orchestra/festwochenchor/elisabeth schwarzkopf/ elsa cavelti/ernst haefliger/otto edelmann

beethoven symphony no 9 in d minor op 125 "choral"

lp issues: japan MF 18862-18863/cetra LO 530/discocorp RR 390

cd issues: arkadia CDLSMH 34006/rodolphe RPC 32522-32524/ music and arts CD 790/tahra FURT 1003/japanese furtwängler centre WFHC 015/audite 95 641

furtwängler talks to henri jaton about beethoven ninth symphony

lp issue: french furtwängler society SWF 7701

cd issue: french furtwängler society SWF 961-962/tahra FURT 1003

The Tahra and Audite issues of the symphony can both be recommended

255 (421)/august 1954/beta film and soundtrack recordings in salzburg felsenreitschule/*film director paul czinner*

wiener philharmoniker/chor der wiener staatsoper/lisa della casa/ elisabeth grümmer/erna berger/anton dermota/cesare siepi/ otto edelmann/deszö ernster/walter berry

mozart don giovanni

vhs video: deutsche grammophon 072 4403

dvd video: deutsche grammophon 073 0199

the recording was made partly during performances and partly under studio conditions

256 (422-424)/30 august 1954/concert recordings in salzburg festspielhaus

wiener philharmoniker

beethoven symphony no 8 in f op 93

lp issues: cetra LO 530/FE 48/discocorp RR 413/japan WFJ 2-3

cd issues: nuova era 013.6310/013.6300/virtupso 269 7172/as-disc AS 115/ orfeo C293 921B/C409 048L

grosse fuge op 133

lp issues: discocorp RR520/cetra FE 40/nippon columbia OZ 7584

cd issues: virtuoso 269 7322/arkadia CDWFE 363/as-disc AS 373/ music and arts CD 520/deutsche grammophon 435 3242/435 3212/ orfeo C409 048L

beethoven symphony no 7 in a op 92

lp issue: movimento musica 01.029

cd issues: nuova era 013.6313/013.6300/foyer CDS 16007/ virtuoso 269 7172/orfeo C293 921B/C409 048L

Orfeo C409 048L conveniently brings together all three works from this final Salzburg Festival concert

257 (425)/19 september 1954/sender freies berlin recording in berlin titania palast

philharmonisches orchester berlin

beethoven symphony no 1 in c op 21

lp issues: movimento musica 08.001/victor (japan) RCL 3333

cd issues: rodolphe RPC 32522-32524/music and arts CD 792/ tahra FURT 1025/german furtwängler society TMK 017198

RCL 3333 was incorrectly dated 15 january 1953; tapes of furtwängler's second symphony, which was also performed at this concert, were erased at the conductor's request

258 (426)/28 september-6 october 1954/hmv sessions in vienna musikvereinsaal/*producer lawrance collingwood*

wiener philharmoniker/martha mödl/leonie rysanek/ margarete klose/ludwig suthaus/ferdinand frantz/gottlob frick/gerda scheyrer/judith hellwig/dagmar schmedes/ rut siewert/erika köth/herta töpper/johanna blatter/ dagmar hermann

wagner die walküre

lp issues: hmv ALP 1257-1261/HQM 1019-1023/FALP 383-387/ QALP 10098-10102/electrola E 90100-90104/WALP 1257-1261/ SME 90100-90102/victor LHMV 900/angel seraphim 6012/ emi 1C149 00675-00679M

cd issues: emi 763 0452/naxos 8.111056-8.111058

THE DISCOGRAPHY OF WILHELM FURTWÄNGLER: ALPHABETICAL BY COMPOSER

Numbers refer to the sessions in the main chronological discography, where full recording details can be found; numbers in brackets indicate an incomplete recording (either fragmentary or individual movements from a work)

JOHANN SEBASTIAN BACH (1685-1750)

brandenburg concerto no 3 in g BWV 1048

004 149

brandenburg concerto no 5 in d BWV 1050

042 149

orchestral suite no 3 in d BWV 1068

106 107

air from the third orchestral suite

002

matthäus-passion BWV 244

137 (189) 243

BELA BARTOK (1881-1945)

violin concerto no 2

219

LUDWIG VAN BEETHOVEN (1770-1827)

symphony no 1 in c op 21

143 198 199 240 257

symphony no 2 in d op 36

104

symphony no 3 in e flat op 55 "eroica"

080 096 141 149 181 198
199 201 202 216 218

symphony no 4 in b flat op 60

062 063 064 129 200 218

symphony no 5 in c minor op 67

001 030 040 065 083 084
150 151 179 235 245 248

symphony no 6 in f op 68 "pastoral"

071 074 083 179 197 247
248

symphony no 7 in a op 92

067 111 128 (168) 206 256

symphony no 8 in f op 93

(014) 111 206 256

symphony no 9 in d minor op 125 "choral"

(006) (011) 025 050 052 (053)
069 153 163 164 170 184
211 212 (252) 253 254

159

beethoven/**piano concerto no 1 in c op 15**

088

piano concerto no 4 in g op 58

067 181

piano concerto no 5 in e flat op 73 "emperor"

158

violin concerto in d op 61

072 089 092 205 210

violin romance no 1 in g op 40

205

violin romance no 2 in f op 50

205

cavatina op 130, arrangement for string orchestra

041

coriolan overture op 62

065 099 175

egmont overture op 84

017 018 084 218

fidelio op 72

(046) (103) 145 221 222

160

beethoven/**grosse fuge op 133, arrangement for string orchestra**

185 256

leonore no 2 overure op 72

077 085 126 139 241

leonore no 3 overture op 72a

075 088 110 111 143 186

HECTOR BERLIOZ (1803-1869)

la damnation de faust

148

marche hongroise from la damnation de faust

004 118

BORIS BLACHER (1903-1975)

concertante musik

244

JOHANNES BRAHMS (1833-1897)

symphony no 1 in c minor op 68

(081) 086 088 098 143 174
183 185 187 210 239

symphony no 2 in d op 73

082 (090) 101 190

symphony no 3 in f op 90

(009) 127 244 246

symphony no 4 in e minor op 98

070 106 107 (109) 120 146

piano concerto no 2 in b flat op 83

056 070

violin concerto in d op 77

125 187

double concerto in a minor op 102

124 183

haydn variations op 56a

070 071 118 141 174 183
245

ein deutsches requiem op 45

087 112 (157)

162

brahms/**hungarian dance no 1 in g minor**

004 119

hungarian dance no 3 in f

003 119

hungarian dance no 10 in e

004 119

ANTON BRUCKNER (1824-1896)

symphony no 4 in e flat "romantic"

(044) 173 175

symphony no 5 in b flat

054 169

symphony no 6 in a

(068)

symphony no 7 in e

(043) (051) 126 161 162

symphony no 8 in c minor

078 116 117 242

symphony no 9 in d minor

076

163

JUAN JOSE CASTRO (1892-1964)

obertura para una opera comica

136

LUIGI CHERUBINI (1760-1842)

anacreon overture

154

CLAUDE DEBUSSY (1862-1918)

nuages et fetes from trois nocturnes

162

ANTONIN DVORAK (1841-1904)

slavonic dance in a flat op 46 no 3

004

WOLFGANG FORTNER (1907-1987)

violin concerto

127

CESAR FRANCK (1822-1890)

symphony in d minor

082 234

WILHELM FURTWÄNGLER (1886-1954)

symphony no 2 in e minor

(100) 105 176 203 204 240

symphonic concerto for piano and orchestra

038 (039)

CHRISTOPH WILLIBALD GLUCK (1714-1787)

alceste overture

055 171 172 238

iphigenie in aulis overture

203 204 238

orfeo ed euridice

160

GEORGE FRIDERIC HANDEL (1685-1759)

concerto grosso in d op 6 no 5

040 244

concerto grosso in d minor op 6 no 10

073 136 141 239

FRANZ JOSEF HAYDN (1732-1809)

symphony no 88 in g

173 177 186

symphony no 94 in g "surprise"

150 154

symphony no 104 in d "london"

136

PAUL HINDEMITH (1895-1963)

die harmonie der welt

201 202 217

konzert für orchester (1925)

141

konzertmusik op 48

005

symphonic metamorphoses on themes of carl maria von weber

091

KARL HOELLER (1907-1972)

cello concerto no 2

126

166

ARTHUR HONEGGER (1892-1955)
mouvement symphonique no 3
185

FRANZ LISZT (1811-1886)
les preludes, symphonic poem
236

GUSTAV MAHLER (1860-1911)
lieder eines fahrenden gesellen: wenn mein schatz hochzeit macht; ging heut morgen übers feld; ich hab ein glühend messer; die zwei blauen augen von meinem schatz
169 196 199

FELIX MENDELSSOHN-BARTHOLDY (1809-1847)
violin concerto in e minor
188 191

hebrides overture
004 113 169

hebrides overture/rehearsal sequence
004

ein sommernachtstraum overture
002 092

WOLFGANG AMADEUS MOZART (1756-1791)

symphony no 39 in e flat K543

073 076

symphony no 40 in g minor K550

075 113 120

double piano concerto in e flat K365

114

piano concerto no 20 in d minor K466

247

piano concerto no 22 in e flat K482

182

sinfonia concertante for violin and viola K364

(013)

serenade for 13 wind in b flat K361

097

serenade in g K525 "eine kleine nachtmusik"

024 119

don giovanni K527

144 213 251 255

die entführung aus dem serail overture K384

018

168

mozart/**le nozze di figaro K492**

214

le nozze di figaro overture K492

018

die zauberflöte K620

121 (147) 165

die zauberflöte K620: o zittre nicht mein lieber sohn: der hölle rache

131

OTTO NICOLAI (1810-1849)

die lustigen weiber von windsor overture

155

ERNST PEPPING (1901-1981)

symphony no 2

067

169

HANS PFITZNER (1869-1949)

symphony in c op 46

122

three palestrina preludes

120

MAURICE RAVEL (1875-1937)

daphnis et chloe: second suite

074

rapsodie espagnole

173 186

valses nobles et sentimentales

207

MAX REGER (1873-1916)

variations and fugue on a theme of mozart

(012)

GIOACHINO ROSSINI (1792-1868)

il barbiere di siviglia overture

019

la gazza ladra overture

004

FRANZ SCHUBERT (1797-1828)

symphony no 8 in b minor D759 "unfinished"

(061)	077	(079)	107	128	(178)
185	188	220	245		

symphony no 9 in c D944 "great"

058	061	140	176	217	220

rosamunde overture D797

004	152	188	220

rosamunde: ballet music no 2

002	130	136

rosamunde: entr'acte no 3

002	075	130	136

HEINZ SCHUBERT (1908-1945)

hymnisches konzert for soloists, organ and orchestra

058

171

ROBERT SCHUMANN (1810-1856)

symphony no 1 in b flat op 38 "spring"

175

symphony no 4 in d minor op 120

209 216

piano concerto in a minor op 54

049

cello concerto

054 (068)

manfred overture op 115

127 156

JEAN SIBELIUS (1865-1957)

violin concerto in d minor op 47

060

en saga op 9

060 150

BEDRICH SMETANA (1824-1884)

the moldau from ma vlast

156

172

JOHANN STRAUSS (1825-1899)

die fledermaus overture

024

kaiserwalzer

(061) 128

JOHANN AND JOSEF STRAUSS

pizzicato polka

131

RICHARD STRAUSS (1864-1949)

don juan

047 057 091 150 162 236
239

metamorphosen

095

sinfonia domestica

072

till eulenspiegels lustige streiche

004 068 178 206 246 247

till eulenspiegels lustige streiche/rehearsal sequence

004

173

richard strauss/**tod und verklärung**

085 128 186

vier letzte lieder: frühling; september; beim schlafengehen; im abendrot

138

orchesterlieder: waldseligkeit; liebeshymnus; verführung; winterliebe

047

IGOR STRAVINSKY (1882-1971)

symphony in three movements

146

le baiser de la fee

210

174

PIOTR TCHAIKOVSKY (1840-1893)

symphony no 4 in f minor op 36

124 152

symphony no 5 in e minor op 64

(016) 193

symphony no 6 in b minor op 74 "pathetique"

037 161

waltz and finale from serenade for strings

130

GIUSEPPE VERDI (1813-1901)

otello

167

RICHARD WAGNER (1813-1883)

der fliegende holländer overture

118 193

götterdämmerung

(029) (052) 135 (192) 230-232

götterdämmerung: siegfrieds rheinfahrt

115 138 193 238

götterdämmerung: siegfrieds trauermarsch

018 115 127 236

götterdämmerung: starke scheite schichtet mir dort

102 138 195

lohengrin

(023)

lohengrin prelude

004 089 125 237

die meistersinger von nürnberg

(031) (036) (066)

die meistersinger von nürnberg overture

048 119 127 (178)

die meistersinger von nürnberg: act three prelude

130

die meistersinger von nürnberg: tanz der lehrbuben

119

176

wagner/**parsifal prelude**

033

parsifal: karfreitagszauber

033 161

das rheingold

026 132 223

siegfried

(028) 134 227-229

siegfried idyll

115 193

tannhäuser

(020) (021)

tannhäuser overture

115 162 200 239

tristan und isolde

(007) (008) (045) (059) (093) 194

tristan und isolde: vorspiel und liebestod

004 032 056 057 138* 188
244 246

**this performance contains vocal version of the liebestod*

die walküre

(022) (027) (034) 133 (180) 224-226
258

die walküre: walkürenritt

118

CARL MARIA VON WEBER (1786-1826)

aufforderung zum tanz, orchestrated by berlioz

015

euryanthe overture

237 245 246

der freischütz

249

der freischütz overture

001 019 074 201 202 237

der freischütz: act three entr'acte

019

oberon overture

130

HUGO WOLF (1860-1903)

lieder: im frühling; elfenlied; lebewohl; schlafendes jesuskind; phänomen; die spröde; die bekehrte; anakreons grab; blumengruss; epiphanias; wie lange schon; was soll der zorn?; nein junger herr; mein liebster hat zu tische; bedeckt mich mit blumen; herr was trägt der boden hier?' in dem schatten meiner locken; mögen alle bösen zungen; wie glänzt der helle mond; wiegenlied im sommer; nachtzauber; die zigeunerin

215

178

MISCELLANEOUS

austrian national anthem

150

swedish national anthem

150

WILHELM FURTWÄNGLER SPEAKS

010	094	108	123	139	142
159	166	206	208	233	240
250	254				

INDEX OF ORCHESTRAS

Numbers refer to the sessions in the main chronological discography, where full recording details can be found

index of orchestras/continued

INDEX OF CHOIRS

Numbers refer to the sessions in the main chronological discography, where full recording details can be found

INDEX OF INSTRUMENTAL SOLOISTS

Numbers refer to the sessions in the main chronological discography, where full recording details can be found

index of instrumental soloists/concluded

INDEX OF VOCAL SOLOISTS

Numbers refer to the sessions in the main chronological discography, where full recording details can be found

index of vocal soloists/continued